THE OFFICIAL

UNITED STATES MINT

™

STATE QUARTERS
© 1998 U.S.MINT

HANDBOOK

THE OFFICIAL

UNITED STATES MINT

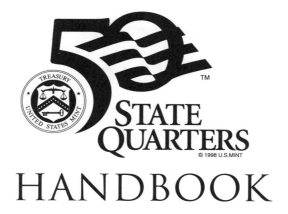

© 1998 U.S.MINT

HANDBOOK

A HISTORY OF

THE MINT,

THE QUARTER &

THE 50 STATES

by
Tricia Boczkowski

LIMITED EDITION

isbn 0-7948-0717-8

The Official United States Mint 50 State Quarters™ Handbook
is a publication of H.E. Harris & Co., that has been developed by The Jim Henson Company under a license from the United States Mint. The 50 State Quarters, the 50 State Quarters logo, and the official Treasury Department/United States Mint seal are trademarks of the United States Mint. All rights reserved.

H.E. Harris & Co.®
Serving the Collector Since 1916

10   9   8   7   6   5   4   3   2   1

FIRST PRINTING

Printed in USA

CONTENTS

MONEY IN AMERICA

EVIDENCE OF THE ORIGIN OF MONEY IN AMERICA dates back as early as 1535. Native Americans used wampum—strings of white beads fashioned from quahog clam shells—as their principal medium of exchange. Most likely, wampum (a Native American word meaning "white") was used as a bartering tool because it was coveted as a means of ornamentation. Beads were either woven into belts or strung on hempen strings more than a foot in length or in much longer strands of about six feet. Worn as an insignia of rank and dignity, the beads were also used as symbolic gifts to mark treaties, ceremonies, and other special occasions.

When the early settlers arrived in the New World, they adopted the practice of using wampum to trade with the Native Americans. Other accepted means of exchange included local products such as beaver skins, furs, and Virginia tobacco. With the influx of immigrants

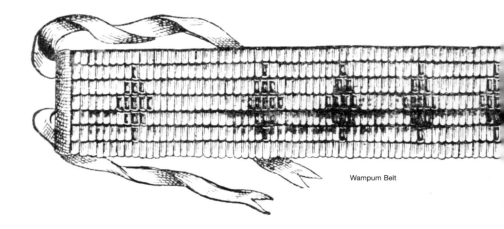

Wampum Belt

from Europe in the seventeenth century, foreign coins of all sorts became accepted forms of payment for goods. The Spanish colonial eight *reales* coin that originated in Mexico, Bolivia, Chile, Colombia, Guatemala, and Peru became the principal monetary unit in the American colonies and was the inspiration for our own silver dollar.

The settlers continually asked the British to provide gold and silver coins to be used in the colonies, but their requests fell on deaf ears. The General Court of the Massachusetts Bay Colony finally took matters into its own hands and granted smith John Hull the authority to begin producing "New

Pine Tree shilling

England" coinage in 1652. Minted in British units to make trade with British merchants easier, Boston's Pine Tree, Oak Tree, and Willow Tree shillings provided the colonists with much-needed currency. Other colonies followed suit, and eventually many different kinds of coins and tokens were produced.

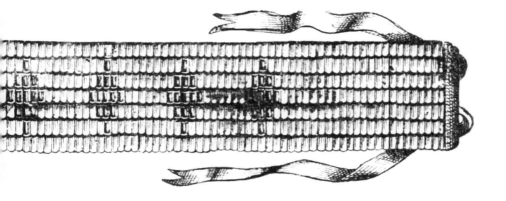

THE U.S. MINT

ONCE INDEPENDENCE FROM ENGLAND WAS SECURED at the end of the Revolutionary War, the framers of the U.S. Constitution called for the creation of a uniform monetary system to be respected by all the states. "The Congress shall have power to coin money, regulate the value thereof, and of foreign coin, and fix the standard of weights and measures," states Article I, Section 8 of the U.S. Constitution. George Washington, Thomas Jefferson, and Alexander Hamilton were the major spokesmen for the establishment of the United States Mint, espousing the view that its creation would give the United States prominence and stature around the world.

In 1784, Thomas Jefferson proposed a decimal system as the basis for American money, advocating the dollar unit as the most familiar, convenient, and simple value to use. Congress approved the basic dollar unit and its decimal ratios the following year, and Secretary of the Treasury, Alexander Hamilton, personally oversaw the planning of a national Mint.

The Philadelphia Mint | On April 2, 1792, Congress authorized the construction of a Mint building in Philadelphia, Pennsylvania, the seat of the U.S. government at the time. This was the first federal building erected under the new Constitution. Even though Philadelphia was only capital of the United States until 1800 (except for 1785–1790 when New York was the temporary capital), an Act of Congress in 1828 directed the Mint to remain permanently in the city. The cornerstone for a larger building, the second Mint, was laid the following year.

As the demand for coinage surpassed the capacity of the second Mint, a third building—the "Grand Old Lady of Spring Street"—was erected in 1901. Described by one observer as "at once a palace of the order appropriate to a structure of the Government, a treasure house, and a workshop and factory of the highest class," the lobby of the building featured seven mosaic panels of Tiffany favril glass, and the workshop employed many manufacturing improvements. Finally, in 1969, the fourth and current Mint was constructed near the site of the very first Mint building and occupies more than five acres of land.

Olde Philadelphia Mint

The Early Years | In 1792, President George Washington appointed David Rittenhouse, a leading American scientist, as the first Director of the U.S. Mint. Harnessed horses were used to drive the crude machinery that produced our coinage. The process involved heating metals in a blacksmithlike furnace and flattening them into sheets by repeated passes through rollers. Coin shapes were then punched out and hand-fed into machines that stamped on coin faces and cut reeded edges. Back then, it took minutes to produce a single cent, and imperfections were frequent. Today's Philadelphia and Denver Mints use a highly automated version of the same process and produce about seven hundred coins per minute.

The Act of 1792 directed American money to be made of gold, silver, and copper. The five dollar, ten dollar, and the two dollar-fifty-cent pieces were minted in gold; the dollar, half-dollar, quarter-dollar, dime, and half-dime were composed of silver; and the cent and half-cent were made of copper. Under Rittenhouse, the Mint produced its first circulating coins in 1793—11,178 copper cents.

Soon thereafter, gold and silver coins were issued as well. (Legend holds that President Washington, who lived only a few blocks from the new Mint, donated some of his personal silver for minting.) The practice of minting from silver and gold continued well into the twentieth century. It was not until 1933, during the Great Depression, that gold coins ceased to be produced, and a silver crisis in 1965 caused the replacement of silver with a copper-nickel coating on a pure copper core in quarters and dimes.

From 1794 to 1834, a negligible amount of quarters, dimes, and half-dimes were produced—an amount insufficient for the needs of commerce, despite the U.S. Mint's efforts to keep up with demand. A new law was passed in 1834 that reduced the weight of standard gold, proving extremely beneficial to both trade and finance.

Get-Rich-Quick Schemes | The Act of 1792 further stipulated that coin defacement, counterfeiting, and embezzlement by Mint employees were offenses punishable by death. According to Mint lore, there have been a handful of creative embezzlement schemes over the course of history, though no death sentences were recorded. A Philadelphia Mint worker, around the turn of the twentieth century, apparently stuffed gold coins down the throat of a dead rat, then tossed it out the window so that he could retrieve the loot undisturbed from the sidewalk after his shift. He got a little too greedy one day, and the overstuffed carcass ruptured upon impact—he was caught red-handed. Some say this is the reason the current Philadelphia Mint was built with no windows that open.

In 1920, a Denver Mint employee was discovered with a stash of 80,000 dollars in gold at his house. He had smuggled most of the coins out of the Mint in his wooden leg. Today, the U.S. Mint scans all employees and visitors with sophisticated monitoring devices upon entering and leaving the building, and runs comprehensive background and security checks on all prospective Mint employees to guard against such thefts.

Civil War Mints | In 1837 and 1838, under President Andrew Jackson, the Mint added three southern branches in New Orleans, Louisiana; Charlotte, North Carolina; and Dahlonega, Georgia, to complement the Philadelphia facility. The discovery of gold in the south in the early 1800s was one of the catalysts for the establishment of these Mints. In fact, the facilities in Charlotte and Dahlonega minted only gold coins.

During the Civil War, all three of the Mints in the South fell under Confederate control, and much of the Mint's machinery was transferred to Confederate gun factories. The South used the New Orleans Mint to produce more than 500,000 dollars in gold and silver Confederate coins, and the Charlotte Mint was used as a Confederate Army headquarters and hospital. Thus the three southern facilities became known as the Civil War Mints.

Western Branch Mints | Similarly, the settling and expansion of the West necessitated the establishment of two branch Mints: one in San Francisco, California, built in 1854 in response to the gold rush of 1849, and the other in Denver, Colorado, in 1862 exclusively for the purpose of minting gold coins. Also, the administrative headquarters moved from Philadelphia to Washington, D.C., in 1873. A host of other Mint outposts were created after the Civil War in such places as Carson City, Nevada; St. Louis, Missouri; Seattle, Washington; Boise, Idaho; Salt Lake City, Utah; and West Point, New York. Many of these branches across the country were closed in the early 1900s. With the advances in technology and transportation that took place around the turn of the twentieth century, there was no longer a need to keep them in operation. The Mint outpost in West Point, New York, is the only one still in working operation.

The San Francisco Mint after the 1906 earthquake

The Granite Lady | The old San Francisco Mint, nicknamed the "Granite Lady" for its stately granite classic Greek revival architecture, survived the great earthquake of 1906. Not only did the building withstand the quake, it saved the city from total economic chaos by serving as a financial hub after much of the area was leveled. Because the sub-treasury and all banks were destroyed in the devastating earthquake and fire, the Mint was the only institution able to manage the receiving and disbursing of relief funds fundamental to the city's recovery. Although the Granite Lady was enveloped in flames, its contents were saved by U.S. Army soldiers and U.S. Mint employees who bravely fought the fire for seven hours.

By the 1930s, the building was deemed inadequate to handle the growing commercial demands of the nation, and the new San Francisco Mint was erected in 1937.

The U.S. Mint Today | Today's U.S. Mint facilities include the Washington, D.C., headquarters, which is responsible for policy making, administrative guidance, and various program operations; the Mints at Philadelphia and Denver which, among other things, manufacture coins of all denominations for general circulation; the San Francisco Mint, which produces silver proof, uncirculated, and commemorative coins; and the West Point Mint, which produces certain silver, gold, platinum, and commemorative coinage. Mint marks appear on every coin produced to designate which U.S. Mint facility issued the coin—an "S," "D," "P," or "W" is stamped onto the obverse (or "heads" side) of each coin.

In addition to these functions, the Mint oversees the U.S. Bullion Depository, located at Fort Knox, Kentucky, where much of our country's gold holdings are stored. No gold has been transferred to or from the depository for many years, except for very small samples used to test its purity during regularly scheduled audits. During World War II, the Declaration of Independence, the U.S. Constitution, and the Bill of Rights were secretly stored in protective vaults at Fort Knox for safekeeping. When Allied victory was imminent in 1944, the documents were returned to Washington, D.C.

Early Coin Design | In the Act of 1792, Congress mandated that all American coins show, on the obverse, "an impression emblematic of Liberty, with an inscription of the word Liberty, and the year of coinage; and upon the reverse (or "tails" side) of each of the gold and silver coins there shall be the figure or representation of an eagle, with this inscription, 'United States of America'..." Various artistic interpretations of Liberty appeared on coins for more than a century before the designs most familiar to us, namely the heads of Presidents Washington, Lincoln, Jefferson, Roosevelt, and Kennedy, were minted.

It was not until 1899 that George Washington's image was placed on a commemorative dollar, with the Marquis de Lafayette. Interestingly, in considering designs for the first U.S. coins, President Washington and Congress rejected designs picturing him. They felt that putting the likeness of a famous U.S. president on our coinage was a practice too closely modeled on the monarchy from which the United States had rebelled.

It was not until 1932 that Washington appeared on the quarter. The portrait of George Washington by John Flanagan, which has been on all quarters since, was originally selected to commemorate the two hundredth anniversary of Washington's birth. This new design was so popular with the American public that, after a year hiatus in 1933, the Washington quarter has been minted each year, with occasional modifications, until the launch of the 50 State Quarters Program™ in 1999.

THE QUARTER

THE SPANISH DOLLAR AND ITS FRACTIONAL PARTS made a lasting impression on coinage in the United States. Americans grew so accustomed to using it during the colonial period that it remained in circulation as legal tender until 1857. Also known as "piece of eight" because the dollar was valued at eight *reales*, the coins were sometimes cut into eight wedges or "bits" when small change was unavailable in the colonies.

"Two bits" were the equivalent of twenty-five cents, hence the centuries-old expression for the quarter. In fact, quarters and half-dollars technically are not under the umbrella of Thomas Jefferson's decimal system. Rather, the two denominations were born of this practice of cutting up the Spanish "piece of eight."

"Two bits"

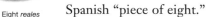

Eight *reales*

The 1796 Quarter | Though authorized by Congress in 1792, the first twenty-five-cent pieces were not manufactured until 1796. A little over six thousand were minted that year, mainly from worn foreign silver coins that were melted down and reused. In keeping with the size and value of foreign coins, like the English shilling and the Spanish-American two *reales*, that had become so familiar to the colonists, the diameter of the first quarter (27.5 mm) was kept almost exactly the same as these predecessors of the twenty-five-cent piece.

It is possible that socialite Ann Bingham served as the model for Miss Liberty on the obverse of the new coin. Fifteen stars appear around her portrait—one for each of the thirteen original colonies, plus Vermont and Kentucky that had since joined the Union—in addition to the word Liberty and the date.

The reverse of the quarter depicts a young eagle, representing our fledgling nation, encircled by a wreath of palm and olive branches, that symbolize peace, and the words United States of America. However, no indication of the coin's value appeared anywhere on the quarter. The oversight was corrected in 1804 when the next batch of quarters was minted—25c. was added to the reverse.

1796 Quarter

The 1804 Quarter | In addition to the inclusion of the denomination on the 1804 quarter, the style of eagle on the reverse changed. A heraldic eagle replaced the 1796 version that depicted the eagle standing on a cloud—this was done so that the quarter would be consistent with the other coins being minted at the time. Also, only thirteen stars, representing the thirteen original colonies, appeared around the bust of Liberty on the obverse of the quarter.

The original intention was to add one star for each state that joined the Union—there were fifteen in 1796. But by 1803, both Tennessee and Ohio had become states, and it was clear that it would not be possible to represent the entire country on one quarter. (Interestingly, the Sacagawea dollar features seventeen stars to repre-

1804 Quarter

sent the number of states in the Union at the time of Louis and Clark's famous expedition.) The 50 State Quarters™ Program has again taken up the cause of recognizing each state's year of statehood with one unique quarter per state.

The 1815 Quarter | After a somewhat slow start, coin production gained momentum in 1815 and has maintained steady output ever since. Another design modification was made to the 1815 quarter: Liberty faced left instead of right and was completely redrawn. The soft and womanly features of Robert Scot's 1796 model were replaced by a stronger, more stoic look in John Reich's 1815 design. He also incorporated the word Liberty into her headpiece rather than printing it above her head.

In addition, the eagle on the reverse appears more lifelike; standing on an olive branch, a symbol of the nation's desire for peace, it clutches three arrows in its talons, a symbol of being ready to defend and fight. Reich's quarter was also the first to carry the motto of the United States—E

1815 Quarter

PLURIBUS UNUM (Latin for "out of many, one")—which was printed in a banner above the eagle's head.

The 1831 Quarter | By 1831, technological advances improved the machinery used by the U.S. Mint, thus improving the quality of the coins themselves. The modern equipment reduced the diameter slightly (to 24.3 mm) and made the quarters perfectly round in shape. To accommodate this new size, Mint engraver William Kneass removed the banner containing the motto and sharpened the lettering and some of the details on the images of Liberty and the eagle.

1831 Quarter

The 1838 Quarter | Seven years after these revisions were made, the quarter was given an entirely new look and composition. Instead of picturing the traditional bust of Liberty, she was shown seated with one hand on the national shield, the other holding a staff and a Phrygian cap. (A Phrygian cap was a cloth hat, which in Roman times, was awarded to slaves upon earning their freedom, and thus came to symbolize liberty.)

The weight of the redesigned quarter also changed in 1838—it was reduced from 6.74 to 6.68 grams, which meant that the percentage of silver had to increase from 0.8924 to 0.90 in order to compensate for the difference in weight. The seated Liberty

1838 Quarter

quarter was minted at the main U.S. Mint in Philadelphia, and the newly opened New Orleans branch Mint.

Minor modifications were made to the seated Liberty design over the course of the next half-century, the most significant being the lowering of the weight to 6.22 grams. By 1853, the price of silver had risen so much that the value of each quarter exceeded twenty-five cents. The U.S. Mint designated the reduced weight of the coin by placing arrows on either side of the date and added rays to the background of the eagle on the reverse to further distinguish the quarter. As the public grew familiar with the look and feel of the new coin, the arrows were removed, and the original eagle design was restored. Another shift in weight occurred in 1873 and 1874—to 6.25 grams—and the arrows were again employed to indicate the increase.

The 1866 Quarter | The other notable change to the quarter's design occurred in 1866 when the phrase IN GOD WE TRUST was printed in a banner above the eagle on the reverse. During the Civil War, when the nation suffered more death and destruction than the two World Wars combined, a minister from Pennsylvania suggested the inclusion of some recognition of God to national coinage as a beacon of faith for our country's citizens. The phrase first appeared on the copper two-cent coins of 1864 and was added to the quarter two years later. In 1955, it became obligatory to include those words on all U.S. currency, and one year later, an act of Congress made IN GOD WE TRUST our national motto. The Mints in San Francisco, Philadelphia, Carson City, and New Orleans all struck versions of the seated Liberty design.

The 1892 Quarter | It was not until 1892 that the allegorical, full-bodied figure of Liberty was again depicted only as a head. Mint engraver Charles Barber designed a more masculine, almost Roman profile on the obverse, with the national motto above the head, and he gave the heraldic eagle spread wings on the reverse. He was the first artist to include his initial "B," which appeared at the base of Liberty's neck. Struck at the Philadelphia, San Francisco, Denver, and New Orleans Mints, the Barber quarter was well received by the public and remained in circulation until 1916.

1892 Quarter

The 1916 and 1917 Quarters | By 1916, World War I was underway and yet another redesign was called for in an effort to reflect the concerns of the day. Herman A. MacNeil, whose initial "M" was printed above the date to the right, chose to show a standing figure of Liberty—left arm raised, shield in hand, in a gesture of protection, and

1916 Quarter   1917 Quarter

right hand clutching an olive branch in a gesture of peace. Despite the beauty of MacNeil's design, it caused a public outcry because Liberty's breast was exposed, and many felt the image to be too risque. She was outfitted with an armor plate the following year as protection of her modesty.

The 1932 Quarter | Finally, in 1932, the familiar image of George Washington's head was introduced to the quarter's design in celebration of the bicentennial of his birth. The artist, John Flanagan's, initials, "JF," appear at the base of the neck on the obverse.

Although intended to be a short-lived commemorative issue, the Washington quarter was so well received that it became a fixture in circulating coinage until 1998. The Mint Act of 1965, however, mandated the use of copper and nickel instead of silver in the quarter's composition, which reduced the quarter's standard weight to 5.670 grams.

1932 Quarter

The 1976 Quarter | The other bicentennial event to be commemorated on the quarter was the anniversary of the signing of the Declaration of Independence. Designed by Jack L. Ahr—the winner of an open contest held by the Treasury—the reverse of the quarter features a colonial drummer in a tricorn hat with a victory torch encased by thirteen stars beside him. Since the production of the Bicentennial quarter in 1975–1976, the first change to the quarter occurred in 1999 with the launch of the 50 State Quarters™ Program.

1976 Quarter

PROGRAM

U PON CONSIDERING THE CHANGES, BOTH SUBTLE and drastic, that America's quarters have undergone over the course of more than two centuries, the ambitious scope of the U.S. Mint 50 State Quarters™ Program becomes wildly apparent. From 1999 to 2008, five newly designed circulating quarters will be issued at ten-week intervals every year by both the Philadelphia and Denver Mints. Annual proof sets (specially made coins distinguished by sharpness of detail) are being produced at the San Francisco Mint.

Released in the order in which the states ratified the U.S. Constitution and joined the Union, the quarters feature a design emblematic of each state's unique history on the reverse. Congress authorized the program on December 1, 1997, with the intent of educating Americans— young and old alike—about our national heritage.

The decision to begin this initiative at the turn of a new century and a new millennium is particularly timely. Such momentous turning points inspire a look at the events that have shaped our past and give us a stronger sense of being part of a larger historical framework. A little over two hundred years ago, we were merely a smattering of loosely linked colonies under royal rule. The extraordinary events of our young country's growth into a strong, democratic nation naturally endow Americans with a strong sense of pride. By celebrating the unique contributions of each state with a series of commemorative quarters, the U.S. Government has provided every citizen with the opportunity to collect a tangible piece of American history.

The design process of the statehood quarters has an equally democratic scope. Each governor determines the submission and selection process—some make their design recommendations by committee, others solicit the opinion of the general public. Concepts are then sent to the U.S. Mint with supporting background reference material. Mint artists produce the drawings of all design concepts that are deemed suitable for coining.

These drawings are reviewed by the Citizens Commemorative Coin Advisory Committee (CCCAC), which is composed of three members of the numismatic community, three members of the general public, and one U.S. Mint employee. The candidate's designs are then reviewed by the Fine Arts Commission (FAC)—a group of seven members elected every four years by the president for the purpose of advising the government on the art and architecture of Washington, D.C., along with the design of coins and medals issued by the U.S. Mint. Between three and five candidates' designs are then sent to the Secretary of the Treasury for review before they are forwarded to the governor for final selection. Final approval is then given by the Secretary of the Treasury before the quarters go into production.

As it is important that dignified designs appear on our national coinage, the U.S. Treasury has set forth criteria to ensure the appropriateness of the selections. Education is

the U.S. Mint's primary focus. As per Public Law 105-124, concepts that promote "the diffusion of knowledge among the youth of the United States about the state, its history and geography, and the rich diversity of our national heritage" are encouraged.

The designs should hold broad appeal and avoid controversial subject matter—suitable subjects include state landmarks, landscapes, historically significant buildings, symbols of state resources or industries, official state flora and fauna, state icons, and outlines of the states.

In order to better accommodate the state designs, Congress passed special legislation on May 29, 1998, to allow four inscriptions on the obverse—UNITED STATES OF AMERICA, LIBERTY, IN GOD WE TRUST, and QUARTER DOLLAR—thereby slightly reducing the size of George Washington's image. Mint Engraver William Cousins executed this modification and his initials flank those of the original designer John Flanagan. All of the quarters' reverses feature the state's name, year of statehood, year of the coin's issue, and E PLURIBUS UNUM, in addition to any other text chosen by the state.

By generating an understanding of the composition of the country's national landscape—from natural resources and landmarks to the people and events that have shaped the nation—the new quarters provide a pocket-size history lesson that engenders pride and respect among our citizens.

New Hampshire

Vermont

Massachusetts

Maine

Minnesota

Wisconsin

Michigan

New York

Rhode Island

Connecticut

New Jersey

Delaware

Maryland

Iowa

Illinois

Indiana

Ohio

Pennsylvania

West Virginia

Virginia

Missouri

Kentucky

North Carolina

Tennessee

South Carolina

Arkansas

Mississippi

Alabama

Georgia

Louisiana

Florida

HISTORY OF

THE FIFTY STATES

DELAWARE

December 7, 1787

Capital: Dover	Area: 1,955 square miles	Motto: Liberty and Independence
Bird: Blue hen chicken	Tree: American holly	Flower: Peach blossom

De La Warr | Among the earliest European explorers to visit Delaware was British captain Sir Samuel Argall. Sailing for Virginia in 1610, he spotted present-day Cape Henlopen and named the waterway after Virginia's first colonial governor, Thomas West, Third Baron De La Warr. Although the cape was renamed, the name *Delaware* was soon applied to the river, the bay, and the surrounding land—even the Lenni-Lenape who inhabited the region were referred to as the Delaware Indians.

In 1682, William Penn, founder of the Pennsylvania colony, was deeded the Three Lower Counties, most of which is now Delaware, by the Duke of York. Delaware sought the establishment of a separate assembly, and in 1704, effectively became a separate colony under the governor of Pennsylvania. Just one month before the thirteen colonies declared independence from the British crown, Delaware formally severed its ties to Pennsylvania and began organizing a state government.

The Ride of Caesar Rodney | During the spring and summer of 1776, the Continental Congress met in Philadelphia to discuss declaring independence from Britain. The three Delaware delegates were Thomas McKean and George Read of New Castle, and Caesar Rodney of

Kent. McKean and Rodney were in favor of independence, but Read felt that breaking from the British Crown was too drastic a measure.

While in Dover, Caesar Rodney received word from Thomas McKean that Congress was going to vote on the issue on July 2. Knowing that Read was opposed to American independence, Rodney rode to Philadelphia as fast as he could to cast the deciding vote for Delaware. It was an agonizing eighty-mile ride through intense heat and torrential downpours. Despite his serious asthmatic condition, Caesar Rodney pushed northward, determined to advocate Delaware's support of the nation's independence.

Mud-soaked and exhausted, he arrived at Independence Hall during the last minutes of debate and supposedly declared, "As I believe the voice of my constituents and of all sensible and honest men is in favor of independence, my own judgment concurs with them. I vote for independence." Rodney's gallop into history meant the Declaration of Independence received unanimous approval from all thirteen colonies.

> **Did You Know?**
> The role of Delaware's state bird, the blue hen chicken, dates back to the Revolutionary War—a company of soldiers from the state brought a number of these cockfighting chickens with them for amusement during lulls in the fighting. Delaware soldiers earned a reputation for being tough in battle and were nicknamed after their equally combative birds.

Statehood | Delawareans were among the most active supporters of the movement for a strong federal government in the United States after the Revolutionary War. Congress called for a constitutional convention to be held in Philadelphia in 1787, and five delegates from Delaware attended the meeting. One of the delegates, statesman John Dickinson, helped frame the U.S. Constitution and later wrote a series of newspaper articles urging its adoption under the pen name Fabius. On December 7, 1787, at a state constitutional convention, the U.S. Constitution was adopted with unanimous approval. Delaware was ahead of all other states in ratifying the document, hence the nickname the *First State*.

PENNSYLVANIA

December 12, 1787

Capital: Harrisburg	**Area:** 44,820 square miles	**Motto:** Virtue, Liberty, and Independence
Bird: Ruffed grouse	**Tree:** Eastern hemlock	**Flower:** Mountain laurel

Penn's Woods | The Commonwealth of Pennsylvania was named in honor of Admiral William Penn. In 1681, King Charles II gave Admiral Penn's son, William, the enormous tract of land west of the Delaware River between New York and Maryland in repayment of a sixteen-thousand pound debt owed to Penn's father before he died. The king insisted on naming the colony after the admiral and because the countryside was dominated by woodland—*sylvania* means "woods" in Latin—it was called Pennsylvania, or Penn's Woods.

William Penn was a member of the Society of Friends, or Quakers, and this new settlement, which he dubbed the Holy Experiment, served as a haven for his fellow persecuted members. He proposed a progressive system of government that advocated religious freedom, fair and humane treatment of Native American tribes, and the establishment of a representative assembly.

Wit and Wisdom | Philadelphia resident Benjamin Franklin was the quintessential Renaissance man—a printer, author, philosopher, scientist, inventor, and statesman. For all of his accomplishments, Benjamin Franklin's most notable contribution was his matchless skill in diplomacy.

> **Did You Know?**
> The Liberty Bell, weighing in at 2,080 pounds, cracked the first time it tolled at a test ringing in Independence Square. It had to be completely recast before it could ring again on July 8, 1776 for the first public reading of the Declaration of Independence. The crack that is still visible in the bell occurred during a celebration of George Washington's birthday in 1846.

A brilliant conversationalist and a sympathetic listener, he won favor with people of all kinds—intellectuals, laymen, and statesmen alike. He successfully bolstered the financial and military support of the French for the American revolutionary cause and was the lead negotiator of the Treaty of Paris that effectively ended the war. Franklin's winning combination of common sense, wit, industry, determination, tact, and tolerance had a pervasive influence on the minds of the American people and on the formation of our democracy.

Statehood | Philadelphia (Greek for "City of Brotherly Love") was host to the Constitutional Convention of 1787. Pennsylvania's revolutionary leaders were opposed to the idea of a strong centralized government. Having just fought to free themselves from England, they feared creating another despotic authority. Nevertheless, the moderates were in the majority and succeeded in ratifying the U.S. Constitution. On December 12, 1787, Pennsylvania became the second state to enter the Union.

NEW JERSEY

THE GARDEN STATE

December 18, 1787

Capital: Trenton	Area: 7,419 square miles	Motto: Liberty and Prosperity
Bird: Eastern goldfinch	Tree: Red oak	Flower: Purple violet

Jersey Roots | Sailing for France, Giovanni da Verrazano was the first European to explore New Jersey in 1524. However, it was Henry Hudson's exploration that opened the region to the Dutch in 1609. After periods of Dutch and Swedish settlement, in 1664 the British took over the area west of the Hudson River and renamed it New Jersey, for the island of Jersey in the English Channel.

King Charles II granted the captured colony to his brother, James, Duke of York, who in turn awarded proprietorship to his friends Lord

General George Washington crossing the Delaware River

John Berkeley and Sir George Carteret. Eager to encourage settlement of their colony, Carteret and Berkeley offered colonists cheap land, representative government, and limited religious freedom—that is, all the residents had to be Protestant.

Crossroads of the Revolution | With more than one hundred battles and skirmishes taking place on New Jersey soil during the Revolutionary War, the state played a central role in the fight for independence. During the harsh winter of 1776, General Washington and his beleaguered troops were desperate for a victory.

The nearest British garrison—consisting mainly of mercenary Hessians—was at Trenton, and Washington decided to launch a surprise attack to catch the enemy off-guard.

On Christmas night, he led his small army across the icy Delaware River to a decisive victory that reenergized the Continental army and boosted American morale. Washington received fresh reinforcements shortly thereafter and made another surprise attack on a British garrison at Princeton, forcing the British to retreat. A victory in Monmouth eighteen months later—the longest running battle of the war—further motivated the rebel army in its fight for freedom.

Statehood | At the Constitutional Convention of 1787, New Jersey proposed a unicameral national legislature in which all states would have equal representation. This proposal came to be known as the New Jersey Plan and was supported by the smaller states. However, large states called for a system based on population. A compromise was reached by giving each state equal representation in the U.S. Senate and population-based representation in the House of Representatives. With the assurance of equality among small and large states in Congress, New Jersey became the third state to ratify the U.S. Constitution on December 18, 1787.

GEORGIA

January 2, 1788

Capital: Atlanta	Area: 59,441 square miles	Motto: Wisdom, Justice, Moderation
Bird: Brown thrasher	Tree: Live oak	Flower: Cherokee rose

Debtor's Colony | Spanish explorer Hernando de Soto led the first European expedition through Georgia in 1540. By the early 1600s, small Spanish settlements, forts, and missions had been established along the coast. After the British founded Charles Town and the Carolina colony in 1670, they began pushing the Spanish southward to Florida. Although the Spanish had abandoned the land by 1686, they continued to fight for possession for more than seventy years.

In 1732, King George II of Great Britain, granted a charter to James Oglethorpe and his associates for a colony to be named Georgia in honor of the king. These new trustees planned to use the land as a refuge for the poor in debtor's prisons and the victims of religious persecution. Although the British Government disliked the idea of a debtor's colony, they were anxious to settle the area before the Spanish in Florida and the French in Louisiana encroached on British turf.

Statehood | The only colony not to send delegates to the First Continental Congress, Georgia took up the revolutionary cause only after the Battles of Lexington and Concord. Revolutionaries from Georgia seized control of their colonial government and sent delegates to the Second Continental Congress in 1776 to sign the Declaration of Independence.

Georgians generally favored a strong central government as they needed protection from the Spanish in Florida and the increasingly hostile Native American community. A state convention was held on January 2, 1788, and representatives voted unanimously in favor of adopting the

U.S. Constitution. The first southern state to ratify the U.S. Constitution, Georgia entered the Union as the fourth state.

The Trail of Tears | Long before Europeans set foot on Georgia soil, Creek and Cherokee Native Americans inhabited the land. In the early 1800s, the Cherokees decided to adopt many practices of the Europeans—they learned to read and write in English, they studied European agricultural practices, domestic arts, and Christianity. A scholar by the name of Sequoya even invented an eighty-five letter alphabet, called Talking Leaves. Within a few years, the Cherokee nation adopted a constitution and began publishing a national newspaper, the *Cherokee Phoenix*, printed in both Cherokee and English.

However, when gold was discovered in northern Georgia, white prospectors, looking to get rich, poured into Native American territory by the thousands and began claiming land. In 1838, soldiers tore 18,000 Cherokees from their homes and forced them at bayonet point on a six-month westward march known as the Trail of Tears. More than 4,000 died en route. Legend holds that every time a Cherokee tear fell during this tragic journey, a white rose sprouted on that spot. In 1916, Georgia designated the Cherokee rose as the state flower.

Did You Know?

The famous Georgia peach is not native to the state—Spanish missionaries introduced the fruit to the coast around 1600. (Ty Cobb, one of the best hitters in baseball history with twelve batting titles to his name, was known as the *Georgia Peach*.)

Sequoya

CONNECTICUT

Capital: Hartford	**Area:** 4,845 square miles	**Motto:** He Who Transplanted Still Sustains
Bird: American robin	**Tree:** White oak	**Flower:** Mountain laurel

Quinnehtukqut | In 1614, Dutch mariner Adriaen Block became the first European to explore Connecticut. The Dutch later settled at the mouth of the Connecticut River and engaged the Native American people in a prosperous fur trade. (The name Connecticut comes from the Native American word *Quinnehtukqut*, meaning "beside the long tidal river.") By the 1630s, English settlers from the Plymouth and Massachusetts Bay colonies began migrating south to establish towns in the fertile river valley.

The colony of Connecticut was formed in 1639 after representa-

The Charter Oak

tives from the three main settlements—Hartford, Windsor, and Wethersfield—met to discuss uniting into a single colony governed by a basic set of laws. Known as the Fundamental Orders, these laws are often considered the first written constitution in history—hence the nickname the *Constitution State*—and were based on the principle that "the foundation of authority is laid in the free consent of the people."

The Charter Oak | The most celebrated event in Connecticut's constitutional history was the Charter Oak incident in 1687. Approved by Charles II in 1662, the Connecticut charter granted the colony the right to govern itself and to expand its boundaries to include New Haven and other coastal towns. When James II succeeded to the throne, he sent Sir Edmund Andros to seize the charter and force Connecticut to submit to his rule.

In Hartford, in the middle of the debate about the fate of the charter, the candles went out, and when they were relit, the document was gone. Captain Joseph Wadsworth had swiped it and hidden it in a nearby oak tree, and Sir Edmund Andros returned to England empty-handed. The Charter Oak, which stood tall until 1856 when a storm felled it, became a symbol of American freedom and independence.

> **Did You Know?**
> West Hartford native Noah Webster completed his monumental *American Dictionary of the English Language* in 1828, the first authority to emphasize American rather than British usage.

Statehood | The Connecticut Compromise, proposed by Roger Sherman at the Constitutional Convention of 1787, resolved the crucial question of national representation in Congress, over which the states had become deadlocked. It gave each state equal representation in the upper house (the Senate), while the lower house (the House of Representatives) would be made up of representatives according to population. On January 9, 1788, Connecticut ratified the U.S. Constitution, becoming the fifth state to enter the Union.

MASSACHUSETTS

February 6, 1788

Capital: Boston	Area: 7,838 square miles	
Motto: By the Sword We Seek Peace, but Peace Only Under Liberty		
Bird: Chickadee	Tree: American elm	Flower: Mayflower

Religious Freedom | English navigator John Cabot made the first recorded expedition to Massachusetts in 1498 while seeking a route to Asia. Massachusetts is a word derived from the name of an Algonquin village. The coastal tract was granted to the Plymouth Company by the king of England in 1606, but the task of settlement fell to a group of religious dissenters known as Pilgrims.

En route to Virginia in search of freedom from persecution by the Church of England, their ship, the *Mayflower*, was blown off course, landing instead in Massachusetts in 1620. The Pilgrims drew up the Mayflower Compact—a covenant with the Plymouth Company that set up a government based on the consent of the governed—and established the Plymouth Colony. In 1629, the Massachusetts Bay Company consisting of another group of dissenters from the Church of England, the Puritans, was also granted a royal charter. The origin of the nickname the *Bay State* comes from the site of the Puritans' colony.

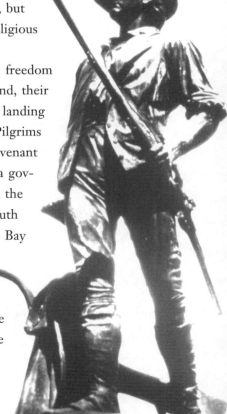

"The Minuteman"

The Shot Heard 'Round the World | A series of events that took place in Massachusetts, namely the Stamp Act riots (1765), the Boston Massacre (1770), and the Boston Tea Party (1773), led to the outbreak of the Revolutionary War. In punishment of the colony's defiance of the Crown, British Parliament passed laws that closed Boston's harbor, revoked the royal charter, and required colonists to house British soldiers. Labeled the "Intolerable Acts" by disgruntled colonists, these laws spurred other colonies to rally in support of Massachusetts.

British troops were sent to Concord to seize ammunition and military supplies in 1775, but local patriots, including Paul Revere, rode through the countryside warning colonial militia. The first shots of the war were fired in Lexington; more minutemen—the name for these militiamen trained to assemble at a minute's notice—amassed in Concord, and forced the British to turn back to Boston. Thousands of colonists rallied throughout the countryside to support the revolutionary cause, and the war for independence was underway.

Statehood | After the Revolutionary War, economic depression set in, and high land taxes were imposed by the merchant-controlled state legislature to offset the cost of the war. In 1786, Daniel Shays led an armed rebellion, consisting mostly of poor farmers in danger of losing their property, to protest these high taxes. Although the rebels were defeated by state militia, Shays' Rebellion encouraged support of a strong central government to deal with such uprisings and also prompted state tax reform.

At first, Massachusetts refused to ratify the U.S. Constitution until a bill of rights that would protect the interests of the individual was included. Although the Bill of Rights was not added until 1791, Massachusetts entered the Union on February 6, 1788, as the sixth state.

Did You Know?

The official state heroine of Massachusetts, Deborah Samson, disguised herself as a man named Richard Shurtleff and fought in the Revolutionary War until her gender was discovered after being wounded in battle.

MARYLAND

THE OLD LINE STATE

April 28, 1788

Capital: Annapolis	Area: 9,775 square miles	Motto: Manly Deeds Womanly Words
Bird: Baltimore oriole	Tree: White oak	Flower: Black-eyed Susan

Lord Baltimore | Explored by Giovanni da Verrazano in 1524, Maryland was eventually settled by the British in 1631, when Virginian William Claiborne built a fur-trading post on Kent Island. A year later, George Calvert (Lord Baltimore), a former high adviser to Charles I, was granted the northern portion of the Virginia colony by the king. His son, the second Lord Baltimore, Cecilius Calvert led a group of Catholics seeking religious freedom to Saint Clements Island in 1634 and established Saint Mary's City. The Maryland colony was named for the wife of King Charles I, Queen Henrietta Maria.

From State House to State Line | Maryland's strategic position along the eastern seaboard contributed to its central role in many of the nation's early political activities. The State House in Annapolis, erected in 1772, saw much of this activity. In addition to housing Maryland's colonial legislature, the building served as the nation's first peacetime capital from 1783 to 1784, and was the site of the signing of the Treaty of Paris that effectively ended the Revolutionary War. The oldest state capital building still in legislative use, the Maryland State House features an impressive wooden dome—the largest in the nation constructed without a single nail.

During the nineteenth century, Maryland's location again placed the state in a pivotal position. The famous Mason-Dixon Line, originally drawn in 1767 to settle a boundary dispute between Maryland and Pennsylvania, was used to designate the division between free states and slave states in debates over the Missouri Compromise in 1820. A border state with ties to both North and South, Maryland was of critical strategic importance to the Union cause during the Civil War.

Statehood | In 1786, a convention of the states was held in Annapolis to discuss the weaknesses of the Articles of Confederation. Maryland called for a centralized federal government that could effectively impose uniform trade regulations. Although only five states—Virginia, New York, New Jersey, Pennsylvania, and Delaware—attended the Annapolis Convention, the gathering precipitated the Constitutional Convention in Philadelphia the following year. On April 28, 1788, Maryland became the seventh state to ratify the U.S. Constitution.

Did You Know?

Francis Scott Key was inspired to write "The Star-Spangled Banner" after witnessing the unsuccessful British attack on Fort McHenry at the entrance to Baltimore Harbor. Our national motto IN GOD WE TRUST derives from the last stanza of his poem.

Maryland State House

SOUTH CAROLINA

THE PALMETTO STATE

May 23, 1788

Capital: Columbia	Area: 31,113 square miles	Motto: Prepared in Mind and Resources
Bird: Carolina wren	Tree: Palmetto	Flower: Yellow jessamine

Carolana | Although the Spanish, led by Francisco Gordillo in 1521, were the first to lay claim to South Carolina, the British ultimately settled the area. In 1629, Charles I gave the region south of Virginia to Sir Robert Heath, who named the land *Carolana* (Latin form of Charles) in honor of the king. Heath, however, never managed to muster enough resources or people to establish a settlement. In 1663, Charles II changed the name to Carolina and gave the land to eight lord proprietors.

Charles Town (now Charleston) was the first English settlement in the province. By the 1680s, the colonists had grown discontented with the governing policies of the lord proprietors and the lack of protection they provided from pirate and Native American attacks. In 1729, the Carolina colony was divided into North and South, and South Carolina officially became a royal province.

Fort Moultrie | South Carolina was among the most restive colonies prior to the Revolutionary War. Emboldened by their wealth and angered by British infringements on their commerce, Charleston's aristocracy and the plantation owners of the lowlands (who were among the richest men in the thirteen colonies) firmly advocated independence. An independent state government was formed in 1776.

Did You Know?

An African-American dialect, known as Gullah, developed on the Sea Islands three hundred years ago. A blend of West African languages and seventeenth-century English, the language was created by slaves managing the isolated rice plantations of the coastal swamplands.

Parapet of Fort Moultrie, 1865

On June 28, 1776, eleven British warships launched an attack on Fort Moultrie on Sullivan's Island in the Charleston Harbor. Cannon fire rained down on the fort, but little damage was done thanks to the pliability of its tough palmetto log structure. The palmetto became the official state tree in 1939.

Statehood | When the Revolutionary War broke out in 1775, the wealthy merchant and planter class of South Carolina retained the hope of avoiding a complete break with England. Despite mounting discontent with the royal authorities, the colony had prospered under British rule. An independent state government was established in 1776 with the intention of eventually reconciling differences with the Crown.

However, sentiments changed when the British occupied Charleston. The majority of South Carolinians gave their support of independence. After the war, South Carolina ceded its lands west of the Appalachian Mountains to the federal government, and on May 23, 1788, it became the eighth state to ratify the U.S. Constitution.

NEW HAMPSHIRE

THE GRANITE STATE

June 21, 1788

Capital: Concord	Area: 9,304 square miles	Motto: Live Free or Die
Bird: Purple finch	Tree: White birch	Flower: Purple lilac

The Granite Grant | English captain Martin Pring made the first recorded visit to New Hampshire in 1603. His writings about the abundant wildlife in the area inspired other expeditions to follow. The first settlements were made in 1623. David Thompson arrived near Rye and set up a trading post for his fishing operation, and Edward Hilton settled in Dover.

Land grants were given to Captain John Mason and Sir Ferdinando Gorges who, in 1629, divided their joint territory at the Piscataqua River. Gorges named the eastern part Maine, and Mason named the western portion New Hampshire, after the English county of Hampshire where he had spent time as a boy. The third English colony to be established in North America, New Hampshire fared much better than Virginia and Massachusetts in its colonizing efforts despite its tiny population. The settlers even helped prevent starvation in the much larger Plymouth settlement by sending shipments of salted cod.

> **Did You Know?**
> Secretary of the Treasury during the Civil War, Salmon Portland Chase, who hails from New Hampshire, introduced paper money to the United States and is honored with a place on the 10,000 dollar bill.

Live Free or Die | When the Revolutionary War broke out, New Hampshire's minutemen made a strong impact, in spite of their comparatively small numbers. John Stark, who had been taught to fight by Native Americans, led New Hampshire soldiers to victory at the Battle of Bunker Hill in 1775. They also fought in the critical Battle of Bennington in

Old Man of the Mountain

1777, and in the turning-point defeat of the British at Saratoga.

John Stark penned the state motto when offering a toast to his former comrades at a reunion for the anniversary of the Battle of Bennington. As he could not attend the reunion due to poor health, Stark sent a toast with his letter of regret—"Live Free or Die; Death Is Not the Worst of Evils." The New Hampshire legislature adopted the motto "Live Free or Die" in 1945. The craggy profile of the Old Man of the Mountain, a granite formation in the White Mountains resembling the profile of a face, has long been wed to this motto as a symbol of the state's self-determination.

Statehood | After a raid on the British armory at Fort William and Mary in New Castle in 1774, a revolutionary New Hampshire congress took over the government and established a provisional constitution. In keeping with the free-thinking spirit of the citizens, the document was not approved until an article retaining the "right to revolution" had been included. Three weeks prior to the signing of the Declaration of Independence, New Hampshire became the first state to proclaim independence from England.

The state constitution, which provided for a bicameral legislature and an executive council, remained in effect until 1784. Once the U.S. Constitution had been drafted, New Hampshire's legislature entered into another long period of debate over the contents. After much controversy, New Hampshire ratified the U.S. Constitution and entered the federal Union as the ninth state on June 21, 1788.

VIRGINIA

THE OLD DOMINION STATE

June 25, 1788

Capital: Richmond	**Area:** 39,598 square miles	**Motto:** Thus Ever To Tyrants
Bird: Cardinal	**Tree:** Dogwood	**Flower:** Dogwood

Jamestown | English explorer John Cabot may have been the first European to lay eyes on Virginia in 1497, but it was not until the spring of 1607 that the region was colonized. Three English ships, the *Susan Constant*, the *Goodspeed*, and the *Discovery*, landed in Jamestown and established the first permanent British settlement in North America. Disease, starvation, and Indian attacks besieged the settlers upon arrival. Although they managed to repulse the first Powhatan attack, they soon proved to be incompetent pioneers.

Poorly equipped and mismanaged, half of the colony was wiped out within a few months. Their situation was so pitiful that the same Indians who had previously attacked the settlers began providing them with food and advice. Captain John Smith emerged as an energetic leader, providing firm guidance to the ailing colony. Virginia, named for the Virgin Queen, Elizabeth I of England, managed to survive the difficult period of colonization and emerged as the most important state in America for nearly two hundred years.

> **Did You Know?**
> Born into slavery on a plantation in Franklin County in 1856, Booker T. Washington became a leading educator. He devoted his energy to furthering black advancement by encouraging fellow African-Americans to uplift themselves through vocational training and economic self-reliance.

The Planter and the Princess | Englishman John Rolfe was instrumental in Jamestown's transformation from a suffering colony to a port of peace and prosperity. He arrived in Virginia in 1610 and became a planter. Two years later, he found a way to hybridize the tobacco plant so as to eliminate the strong, bitter taste from the leaves. This discovery finally gave the settlers a desperately needed cash crop. They began growing tobacco everywhere, even in the streets of Jamestown; it soon became Virginia's staple crop and brought prosperity to the colony.

John Rolfe also facilitated a period of peace with the local Native Americans through his marriage to Chief Powhatan's daughter, Pocahontas, in 1614. Their union assured peaceful relations between the colonists and the tribe until the deaths of the chief and his daughter.

Statehood | Virginia was at the forefront of the movement for independence from England, and because of the state's size and influence, it was essential that enough differences of opinion be sorted out to ratify the U.S. Constitution. The debate was long and heated, but on June 25, 1788, Virginia approved the document by a narrow margin, with assurances that a Bill of Rights would be incorporated later, and became the tenth state to enter the Union.

Jamestown

NEW YORK

THE EMPIRE STATE

July 26, 1788

Capital: Albany	Area: 49,576 square miles	Motto: Ever Upward
Bird: Bluebird	Tree: Sugar maple	Flower: Rose

What a Bargain | Englishman Henry Hudson sailed up the river that now bears his name as far as present-day Albany in 1609 and inspired his Dutch employers to send fur traders and settlers in his wake. The first settlements in New York—Fort Orange and New Amsterdam—were made in 1624 by the Dutch West India Company. Two years later, Peter Minuit, the governor of the colony (called New Netherland) made what is perhaps the wisest purchase in history when he bought Manhattan from the local Native Americans for trinkets valued at approximately twenty-four dollars.

> **Did You Know?**
> Governor DeWitt Clinton launched the massive project of creating a waterway to link the Hudson River and the Great Lakes in 1817. Dubbed "Clinton's Ditch," the Erie Canal is three hundred forty miles long and took eight years to complete.

By 1664, the Dutch colony was completely taken over by the English. King Charles II granted the land to his brother James, Duke of York. Fort Orange was renamed Albany, while New Amsterdam and New Netherland were called New York.

Statehood | Many New Yorkers were opposed to a strong federal government. At a state convention in 1788, those in favor of ratification of the U.S. Constitution were outnumbered nineteen to twenty-seven. However, two prominent statesmen, Alexander Hamilton and John Jay, launched a skillful campaign to bolster support for joining the Union. They published a series of articles known as *The Federalist* spelling out the benefits of a powerful national government. After New Hampshire entered the Union in June of 1788, New York faced isolation if it did not follow suit. On July 26, 1788, New York became the eleventh state to ratify the U.S. Constitution.

Gateway to Freedom | In 1892, Ellis Island was opened in the New York Harbor as the principal federal immigration station in the United States. New arrivals had to undergo a series of medical and legal examinations before they were allowed to enter the country. During the forty-two years of Ellis Island's use as an immigration station, about twelve million steerage and steamship passengers passed through its doors. An estimated forty percent of the current population in the United States can trace their ancestors back to Ellis Island.

Conditions were often rough for the immigrants. Having sustained long and difficult journeys on overcrowded ships, they were then crammed into halls to nervously await inspection. But the inspiring site of the Statue of Liberty just across the river, provided them with a constant reminder of the dreams they came to fulfill in America.

Immigrants at Ellis Island

NORTH CAROLINA

THE TAR HEEL STATE

November 21, 1789

Capital: Raleigh	Area: 48,718 square miles	Motto: To Be Rather Than to Seem
Bird: Cardinal	Tree: Pine	Flower: Dogwood

Mystery of the Lost Colony | Giovanni da Verrazano was the first European to explore the North Carolina coast in 1524. But it was Englishman Sir Walter Raleigh who claimed Roanoke Island in 1584 as the site of the first British colony. The first attempt at colonization was unsuccessful, and all but eighteen men returned to England after just one year on the island.

John White was sent back to Roanoke Island with a new group of settlers, but the eighteen men who stayed behind had perished. Shortly after the birth of his granddaughter, Virginia Dare, who was the first

Wright Brothers at Kitty Hawk

child of English parents born in America, White went to England to gather supplies. He was detained there for three years and when he finally returned, all of the colonists had disappeared—the mystery of the "lost colony" has never been solved.

Statehood | During the Revolutionary War, North Carolina unanimously ratified the Articles of Confederation. However, when the war ended and it came time to vote on the creation of a much stronger federal government as proposed in the U.S. Constitution, the state declined ratification, requesting several amendments along with a Bill of Rights. After a time, North Carolina grew uncomfortable in its position outside of the federal government, and on November 21, 1789, ratified the U.S. Constitution, making it the twelfth state to join the Union.

> **Did You Know?**
> The origins of the nickname Tar Heel State are disputed—some believe it refers to the fact that tar was the state's major product of the colonial period, others attribute it to the stick-to-itiveness of North Carolina's Confederate troops during the Civil War.

First in Flight | Wilbur and Orville Wright of Dayton, Ohio, opened a bicycle shop in 1892. The brothers were endowed with intuitive mechanical ability and analytical intelligence, and soon turned their attention to a loftier pursuit, the dream of flight. They believed they had as much chance as anyone of succeeding, and began researching, designing, and learning to fly various lighter-than-air machines.

In 1900, the Wrights chose Kitty Hawk, North Carolina, as the site to test their first craft—a kite with a seventeen-foot wingspan that could carry a pilot. When the kite flew well and Wilbur was airborne for a few seconds, they graduated to a wooden, winged sled that also brought encouraging results. The brothers continued to refine their designs until they came up with the Wright biplane, an aircraft with a twelve-horsepower engine and an efficient propeller that they crafted themselves. On December 17, 1903 at Kill Devil Hills near Kitty Hawk, Orville made the first successful flight, which lasted twelve seconds.

RHODE ISLAND

THE OCEAN STATE

May 29, 1790

Capital: Providence	Area: 1,045 square miles	Motto: Hope
Bird: Rhode Island red chicken	Tree: Red maple	Flower: Violet

From Rhodes to Red Island | There is some disagreement over the origins of the name Rhode Island. One opinion is that, in 1524, Italian navigator Giovanni da Verrazano compared Block Island to Rhodes and spawned the name Rhode Island. Others claim that it comes from the Dutch *Roodt Eylandt*, meaning "red island," from the time Dutch navigator Adriaen Block first sailed by the red clay of the island's shores. But it was Englishman Roger Williams who founded the colony. He established the first permanent settlement in Providence and officially named the colony Rhode Island, in 1644, upon obtaining a colonial charter.

Roger Williams | Roger Williams, a Puritan clergyman, immigrated to Boston in 1631. Soon thereafter, he clashed with the Puritan authorities of the Massachusetts Bay and Plymouth colonies. An outspoken advocate of religious freedom, he challenged their right to regulate religious matters, and spoke emphatically against the illegal appropriation of Native American lands on the basis of a royal charter.

In 1635, Roger Williams was banished from Massachusetts and he fled to Narragansett Bay. A year later, he purchased land from the Narragansett tribe and, together with friends from Salem, established Providence. The Native Americans respected Williams highly. He treated them with kindness,

> **Did You Know?**
> On June 27, 1898, after a 46,000-mile journey that lasted three years, Captain Joshua Slocum sailed his sloop into Newport and became the first man to sail around the world solo.

Roger Williams with the Narragansett

learned their language, and always dealt fairly and honestly with them. Thomas Jefferson and John Adams later acknowledged Roger Williams as the originator of the First Amendment principles—freedom of religion, freedom of speech, and freedom of public assembly.

Statehood | Following the Revolutionary War, many Rhode Islanders were opposed to the creation of a strong federal union of the states. The farmer population in Rhode Island wanted to keep local autonomy and preserve states' rights. They preferred to pay their debts with cheap, paper money, and feared that a Federalist government would demand money backed by gold reserves.

There was also a sizable Quaker community in the state that firmly opposed the compromises on slavery that were written into the first U.S. Constitution. Rhode Island did not send any delegates to the Constitutional Convention in 1787. The last of the original thirteen colonies to ratify the U.S. Constitution, Rhode Island entered the Union by the narrowest margin of any state on May 29, 1790. Interestingly, the official state name is actually Rhode Island and Providence Plantations.

VERMONT

March 4, 1791

Capital: Montpelier	Area: 9,249 square miles	Motto: Freedom and Unity
Bird: Hermit thrush	Tree: Sugar maple	Flower: Red clover

Champlain, Champlain | In 1609, Frenchman Samuel de Champlain, the first European known to have explored Vermont, reached the lake that now bears his name. The name Vermont is a derivation of the French words *vert* (green) and *mont* (mountain), hence the nickname *Green Mountain State*. Champlain claimed the region for France; however, no settlements were made in the area for more than one hundred years. The British established the first settlement in 1724 on the site of present-day Brattleboro. The battle between France and England for control of North America went on for many years and was often fought on Vermont soil.

The Green Mountain Boys | New York was granted jurisdiction over Vermont by the English king in 1764. By that time, half of the land in the region had already been sold by the governor of New Hampshire. New York threatened to forcibly remove all landowners who refused to comply with their demands of reimbursement. Land speculator Ethan Allen, his brothers Ira and Levi, and Seth Warner organized local militias to fight New Yorkers who came to enforce the court order. Known as the Green Mountain Boys, they withstood raids and threats for five years until the outbreak of the Revolutionary War redirected their hostilities.

Did You Know?
Born on July 4, 1872, in Plymouth, President Calvin Coolidge earned the nickname "Silent Cal" for his typical Vermonter's reluctance to waste words. When asked by his wife if he would accept the nomination for vice president, his only response was, "Suppose I'll have to."

In addition to capturing Fort Ticonderoga and Crown Point, the Green Mountain Boys played a critical role in the defeat of the British army at the Battles of Hubbardton, Bennington, and Saratoga. As noted by British General John Burgoyne shortly before surrendering, Vermont "now abounds in the most active and rebellious race on the continent, and hangs like a gathering storm on my left."

Statehood | On January 15, 1777, Vermont declared independence from Britain and established a separate republic. Six months later, delegates drafted a liberal constitution—the first in America to prohibit slavery and the first to give all adult males, regardless of property ownership, the right to vote.

The Republic of Vermont lasted fourteen years. However, the period was marked by discord, political rivalries, and ongoing conflict with neighboring states. When the U.S. Constitution was adopted in 1789, Congress looked more favorably upon allowing Vermont to enter the Union. One year later, New York relinquished its claims in exchange for money, and on March 4, 1791, Vermont became the fourteenth state.

The Green Mountain Boys

KENTUCKY

June 1, 1792

Capital: Frankfort	**Area:** 39,732 square miles	**Motto:** United We Stand, Divided We Fall
Bird: Cardinal	**Tree:** Tulip poplar	**Flower:** Goldenrod

Mind the Gap | Both the French and the English made claims on Kentucky (a Cherokee word meaning "meadowland") in the late-seventeenth century. Gabriel Arthur and other English explorers were dispatched westward from Virginia and arrived in Kentucky in 1674. Frenchman René-Robert Cavelier, Sieur de La Salle, traveled south along the Mississippi River, reaching the region in 1682. However, neither country made any attempts to secure its position in Kentucky until the first few decades of the eighteenth century.

In 1750, explorer Thomas Walker from Virginia discovered a pass through the Appalachian Mountains, the Cumberland Gap, that would later become a main route for settlers traveling inland from the coast. However, English settlement of Kentucky was more or less put on hold because of the French and Indian War.

Daniel Boone

Boone Docks | The French and Indian War ended in 1763 and England won all of the territory east of the Mississippi. Native American raids abated in the wake of the war, and hunters began extending their hunting trips into frontier adventures. Daniel Boone was one such "long hunter." He made his first trip to Kentucky in 1767 to hunt, trap, and find a path to the fertile Bluegrass region of which he had heard.

In 1769, Boone crossed the Cumberland Gap and followed the Native American warrior's path to northern Kentucky. He later blazed a trail from the Cumberland Gap to the Bluegrass area of central Kentucky. Known as Boone's Trace, it eventually became part of the famed Wilderness Trail. Once the route was cleared, Boone began leading land-hungry pioneers to the Kentucky frontier and defending them against Native American attack. Tales of his bravery and cunning on these expeditions have circulated for centuries.

> **Did You Know?**
> The nickname *Bluegrass State* comes from the bluegrass in the pastures of central Kentucky—though the grass itself is green, the purple-blue tint of the buds give the pastures a bluish hue when seen from afar.

Statehood | When the Revolutionary War ended, thousands of easterners migrated to Kentucky and the increase in population heightened the demands for separation from Virginia. Nine conventions were held during the period from 1784 to 1790 to resolve issues related to the terms of separation. Once the terms were accepted and Congress had been petitioned for statehood, delegates drafted a state constitution in 1792. Kentucky entered the Union on June 1, 1792 as the fifteenth state and the first state west of the Appalachian Mountains.

Upon achieving statehood, Kentucky became a strong proponent of the frontier point of view, taking a democratic, anti-British, anti-privilege stance. The second state constitution, ratified in 1800, provided for the election of the governor and the senate by popular vote, a provision that other new states later built into their own constitutions.

TENNESSEE

THE VOLUNTEER STATE

June 1, 1796

Capital: Nashville	Area: 42,144 square miles	Motto: Agriculture and Commerce
Bird: Mockingbird	Tree: Tulip poplar	Flower: Iris

Tanasi | In 1540, the Spanish explorer Hernando de Soto ventured to Tennessee (which comes from *Tanasi*, the Cherokee name for the Tennessee River) en route to the Mississippi River. Juan Pardo followed twenty years later and set up several forts in eastern Tennessee. The Spanish abandoned the area completely after a short time, but the diseases they carried from Europe devastated the Native American population.

By the time the French and English arrived in Tennessee in 1673, the area was sparsely populated. A number of explorers and fur traders from both France and England came through Tennessee in the late seventeenth century. When the French lost all of their land holdings to the British in the French and Indian War, back-country settlers in Virginia and North Carolina initiated the first wave of settlement along the Watauga River of Tennessee.

Did You Know?
Nashville's Grand Ole Opry has been broadcast every Friday and Saturday night since 1925, making it the longest running live radio program in the world.

Statehood | In 1789, North Carolina ceded its western land claims to the federal government. The following year, Congress categorized the region as the Southwest Territory and appointed William Blount governor. Voters then chose a legislature that began preparing for statehood.

In 1795, a special census showed that the population, which was predominantly English, German, and Scots–Irish, far exceeded the amount of people necessary to achieve statehood, so Tennessee set about drafting a con-

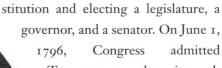

stitution and electing a legislature, a governor, and a senator. On June 1, 1796, Congress admitted Tennessee as the sixteenth state in the federal Union.

Andrew Jackson

Seventh president of the United States and the first man west of the Appalachian Mountains to be elected to the office, Andrew Jackson settled in the frontier village of Nashville as a young man. He had to fight his way through the ranks in politics and struggle to attain wealth in the rough-hewn frontier society of Tennessee. But these obstacles he overcame turned him into a hero of the common people. His landslide victories in the elections of 1828 and 1832 marked the end of the reign of aristocrats from Virginia and New England, and the beginning of the people's Democratic Party.

Jackson's campaign appealed to a wide audience and attracted a broader voting population than prior presidents, who tended to cater to special interest groups. However, Jackson clearly did not include Native or African-Americans in his appeals to the common people. His Indian removal policy was ruthless and brutal, and his siding with proslavery advocates in Congress contributed to the division over slavery that later erupted into the Civil War. Nonetheless, Jackson left a legacy of a strong presidency that had the interests of the common man in mind.

OHIO

THE BUCKEYE STATE

March 1, 1803

Capital: Columbus	Area: 41,222 square miles	Motto: With God, All Things Are Possible
Bird: Cardinal	Tree: Buckeye	Flower: Scarlet carnation

Beautiful River | French explorer Louis Jolliet was the first European known to have reached Ohio in 1669, and René-Robert Cavelier, Sieur de La Salle, is credited with the discovery of the Ohio River in 1670. The name Ohio comes from an Iroquois word meaning "beautiful river." Fifteen years later, English fur-trading expeditions arrived in the region, and tensions rose between the two nations as they vied for control of the profitable fur trade with the Native Americans of Ohio.

Incensed by the loss of trading opportunities, the French organized a group of Native Americans to raid the English fort and trading post at Pickawillany in 1752. Ultimately, these raids and disputes culminated in the French and Indian War.

Statehood | As territorial delegate to Congress, William Henry Harrison pushed through a bill in 1800 that divided the Northwest Territory into east and west. The eastern side retained the name Northwest Territory with boundaries approximating present-day Ohio, and the western side became the Indiana Territory. By 1802, the population of the Northwest Territory had grown substantially, and under an act signed by President Thomas Jefferson, delegates were chosen to draw up a constitution. Renamed Ohio after its western boundary was slightly redefined, it became the Union's seventeenth state on March 1, 1803.

> **Did You Know?**
> Cleveland was originally spelled *Cleaveland* after the leader of the party of surveyors who measured the land. But an early newspaper had to cut one letter from the name to fit it on the front page.

Bright Ideas | Born in Milan, Ohio, in 1847, self-taught genius Thomas Alva Edison was one of the most prolific inventors in history. "Remember," he once said, "nothing that's good works by itself, just to please you. You've got to make the damn thing work." He is credited with more than one thousand patented inventions, including the incandescent electric lamp, the phonograph, the motion picture projector, the carbon telephone transmitter, and the first central electric-power station.

But Edison's most significant contribution was, perhaps, his invention workshops, forerunners to the modern industrial research laboratory. Teams of scientists and engineers collaborated at his "factories" in Menlo Park and West Orange, New Jersey, systematically investigating problems and theories. Edison consciously directed his attention to inventing devices that would have commercial utility and satisfy real needs.

Edison in his laboratory

LOUISIANA

THE PELICAN STATE

April 30, 1812

Capital: Baton Rouge	Area: 43,566 square miles	Motto: Union, Justice, and Confidence
Bird: Eastern brown pelican	Tree: Bald cypress	Flower: Magnolia

Secret Handshakes | Spanish explorer Hernando de Soto was the first European to pass through Louisiana in 1542. One hundred fifty years later, Frenchman René-Robert Cavelier, Sieur de La Salle, made his way down the Mississippi River and claimed a vast region in the name of King Louis XIV, calling it *Louisiane*. The French were the first to settle the region at the start of the eighteenth century.

Louisiane remained a French colony until 1762, when it was signed over to Spain in the secret Treaty of Fontainebleau and renamed *Luisiana*. With the exception of West Florida, Spain gave the colony back to France in another secret treaty in 1800. It was then sold to the United States in 1803 in what is known as the Louisiana Purchase.

Did You Know?
The large Cajun population in Louisiana is attributed to the migration of their ancestors, the Acadians, who were driven from Canada in the eighteenth century because of their refusal to pledge allegiance to the British Crown.

Creole Culture | New Orleans retains the flavor of the various cultural influences that were introduced into the city throughout its history. As a result of the colony being passed back and forth between the French and the Spanish throughout its early history, a French–Spanish culture known as Creole, with its own unique customs and cuisine, was spawned. A significant Catholic heritage also developed in New Orleans during this period, and Mardi Gras festivities still ignite the city annually.

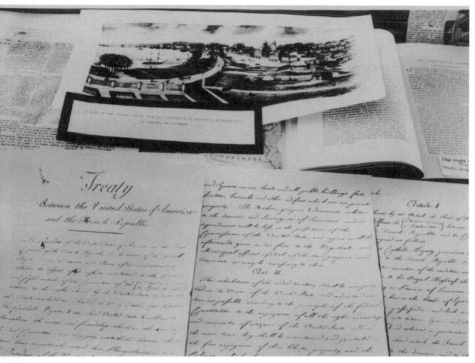

Louisiana Purchase

The African-American population of New Orleans had a major impact on the city as well. A slave uprising in Haiti brought boatloads of people to New Orleans in 1790; the blacks from the West Indies introduced voodoo into Creole culture, along with the music and dance of Haiti. World-famous New Orleans jazz sprang from the lively combination of Haitian rhythms with those of the African-American people.

Statehood | In 1804, Louisiana split into the Territory of Louisiana to the north (in present-day Missouri) and the Territory of Orleans to the south. William C. Claiborne became the territorial governor of the Territory of Orleans and took on the challenge of introducing American democracy to an area that had little experience with self-rule. On April 30, 1812, the Territory of Orleans officially became Louisiana and entered the federal Union as the eighteenth state.

INDIANA

THE HOOSIER STATE

December 11, 1816

Capital: Indianapolis	Area: 35,870 square miles	Motto: The Crossroads of America
Bird: Cardinal	Tree: Tulip poplar	Flower: Peony

Land of the Indians | After René-Robert Cavelier, Sieur de La Salle, first passed through northern Indiana in 1679, the French befriended the local Native Americans and engaged them in a lucrative fur trade. The name Indiana means simply "land of the Indians," in reference to the large population of Native Americans in the region. By 1715, the French had set up fortified trading posts near present-day Fort Wayne and Lafayette; the first permanent settlement at Vincennes was established about ten years later.

After the French and Indian War, the British gained the French land claims in Indiana. However, the Native Americans resented the arrogant British traders and feared that British settlers would soon

Chief Pontiac in council

encroach on their lands. They launched an armed campaign, in 1763, to drive them out of the region. Known as Pontiac's War, the conflict resulted in the capture of seven British trading posts. But Chief Pontiac was unsuccessful in conquering Fort Detroit and had to give up his siege. A peace agreement was finally reached in 1765.

Statehood | In 1800, William Henry Harrison became governor of the huge Indiana Territory, which included all of present-day Indiana, Michigan, Wisconsin, Illinois, and parts of Minnesota. Gradually, these areas split off into their respective territories, and even though the size of the Indiana Territory was significantly reduced, its population grew tremendously during the first few years of the nineteenth century.

> **Did You Know?**
> The origin of the nickname *Hoosier* is disputed—some say it refered to the many Indiana residents hired by contractor Sam Hoosier, others say it came from "hoozer," which means "hill-dweller" in the Cumberland dialect of northwestern England, and still others believe it to be a corruption of the pioneer question, "Who's here?"

The War of 1812 and various uprisings by Native Americans trying to reclaim their lands, slowed Indiana's momentum toward statehood. However, in 1815, the territorial legislature drew up a petition that was approved by Congress and drafted the first state constitution. Indiana entered the federal Union as the nineteenth state on December 11, 1816.

Crossroads of America | Indiana's central location, level terrain, and wide rivers all contributed to the state's motto, "The Crossroads of America." When Indiana first became a state in 1816, it began investing in the construction of canals, railroads, and highways. The Cumberland Road, the country's first major east–west roadway, passed through Indiana, as did an important north–south road that linked Lake Michigan to the Ohio River. The Wabash and Erie Canal provided a route to eastern markets, and extensive railroads were later constructed in the state. This strong transportation network gave Indiana easy access to an ever-expanding national market for agricultural products.

MISSISSIPPI

Capital: Jackson	Area: 46,914 square miles	Motto: By Valor and Arms
Bird: Mockingbird	Tree: Magnolia	Flower: Magnolia

Mississippi Bubble | Spanish explorer Hernando de Soto led the first European expedition across northern Mississippi (an Algonquin word meaning "big river") in 1540. The French came through the region one hundred thirty years later, and René-Robert Cavelier, Sieur de La Salle, included Mississippi in his claim of the vast region called *Louisiane*. Forts and settlements were established along the Gulf Coast and in the Mississippi Valley, and Biloxi became the first permanent settlement in the area.

The French colony struggled at the beginning of the eighteenth century, and in 1717, Scottish financier John Law was given the right to develop the area. He established the French national bank and, to maintain public confidence in the bank, released promotional literature promising quick profits in mining and other endeavors to entice immigrants to settle the region. The colonial government was ill-equipped to handle the massive influx of people, who were mostly indentured servants, convicts, and slaves. The settlers faced brutal conditions upon arrival, many died for want of food, clothing, and shelter. Those who survived only stayed because they were too poor to return home. John Law's settlement plan came to be known as the Mississippi Bubble.

Statehood | When West Florida proclaimed independence from Spanish rule, its eastern half (present-day Alabama) was

> **Did You Know?**
> Otherwise known as "Old Man River," the Mississippi River is the largest in the United States and serves as the nation's principal waterway.

added to the Mississippi Territory. Settlers in the Natchez region began vying for statehood; however, the people in the eastern part of the territory feared that the interests of the wealthy Natchez population would dominate the government if statehood were granted. In 1817, Congress accommodated the easterners by creating the Alabama Territory, and Mississippi entered the federal Union on December 10 as the twentieth state.

Father of the Confederacy | From 1861 to 1865, Jefferson Davis was the first and only president of the Confederate States of America. When Davis was elected to Congress as Mississippi's senator, the former planter often spoke out in favor of slavery and prioritized state's rights. As secretary of war under Franklin Pierce, he was influential in persuading the president to sign the Kansas-Nebraska Act—a measure that favored Southern interests and deepened the rift between North and South.

Jefferson Davis opposed the idea of secession from the Union. However, he was not willing to sacrifice Southern principles in exchange for national solidarity, and he withdrew from the Senate when Mississippi seceded. Davis was elected to the office of provisional president of the Confederate States by popular vote in 1861. Although he was often in conflict with various factions of the Confederacy, he did manage to raise a tenacious army, with General Robert E. Lee at the helm, and to inspire dedication to the cause with his energetic zeal and unwavering faith.

Jefferson Davis

ILLINOIS

THE PRAIRIE STATE

December 3, 1818

Capital: Springfield	**Area:** 55,593 square miles	**Motto:** State Sovereignty, National Union
	Bird: Cardinal	**Tree:** White oak	**Flower:** Native violet

Illini | The French were the first Europeans to set foot in Illinois—explorer Louis Jolliet and Catholic missionary Père Jacques Marquette arrived via the Mississippi River in 1673. Marquette started a mission among the Kaskaskia tribe a year later and others soon sprouted up in the area. The first permanent settlement was Cahokia, a French mission founded in 1699. For the better part of a century, the British, the French, and the Iroquois Confederacy fought for control of Illinois. The name Illinois is the French pronunciation of *Illini*, meaning "the people." The Native Americans used it to describe the six tribes that formed a loose confederacy in the region.

Finally, in 1744, British Parliament passed the Quebec Act, which designated present-day Illinois as part of the French province of Quebec. British colonists were outraged by the legislation, considering it to be one of the so-called "Intolerable Acts." Illinois was returned to the British after the French and Indian War in 1763.

> **Did You Know?**
> The Great Chicago Fire of 1871 killed almost three hundred people, destroyed 17,450 buildings, and triggered forest fires as far away as Michigan and Wisconsin.

Statehood | During the War of 1812, Fort Dearborn, a settlement on the site of present-day Chicago, was destroyed by the British and their Native American allies. Although the fort was rebuilt and strongly garrisoned after the war, the emigrants who arrived by the thousands from Virginia, Kentucky, and other southern states settled in southern Illinois

where the woodlands resembled the landscapes of their home states. The prerequisite for admission to the Union was a population of sixty thousand. Although the Illinois Territory was short by five thousand, it was admitted to the Union on December 3, 1818 as the twenty-first state.

Land of Lincoln | Born in Kentucky in 1809, Abraham Lincoln moved to a farm in Illinois in 1830. He had little formal schooling, but managed to teach himself mathematics and law, as well as literature and poetry. Lincoln became a successful lawyer and worked the Illinois court circuit from 1849 to 1860.

In 1858, he challenged Stephen Douglas for reelection to the Senate. During their famous debate on the issue of slavery, Lincoln spoke out firmly and convincingly: "A house divided by itself cannot stand." Douglas won the election, but Lincoln gained national attention with his eloquent and powerful speeches and became president of the United States two years later.

As president, he issued the Emancipation Proclamation in January, 1863 in the thick of the Civil War, declaring the rebelling states' slaves free. Ten months later, he delivered his noble and moving Gettysburg Address in memory of those soldiers who had died trying to preserve the ideals of a "nation, conceived in liberty and dedicated to the proposition that all men are created equal." Abraham Lincoln was assassinated by John Wilkes Booth on April 14, 1865, eight months shy of the ratification of the Thirteenth Amendment, which ended slavery.

ALABAMA

December 14, 1819

Capital: Montgomery	Area: 50,750 square miles	Motto: We Dare Defend Our Rights
Bird: Yellowhammer	Tree: Southern pine	Flower: Camellia

Golden City | Searching for a kingdom rich in gold that was rumored to exist in the area, Hernando de Soto reached Alabama in 1539 with hundreds of Spanish soldiers in tow. However, by the time the expedition reached Mississippi, their numbers had been greatly reduced by battle, hunger, and disease. De Soto died near the Mississippi River, and after his death, few attempts were made by the Spanish to settle the area.

68

The first Europeans to meet with colonizing success in Alabama were the French. (Alabama is a blend of two Choctaw words meaning "vegetation gatherer.") They set up fortified trading posts up and down the Mobile River, the first one at Fort Louis de la Louisiane.

Did You Know?
The first blind and deaf person to effectively communicate with the sighted and hearing world, Alabama native Helen Keller spoke her first word—water—at the age of seven, while standing at a pump in Tuscumbia with her teacher Annie Sullivan.

Statehood | Alabama was a part of the Mississippi Territory until 1817. By then, so many people had moved to the eastern part of the territory (in present-day Alabama) that settlers in the Natchez region of Mississippi grew increasingly uncomfortable. They had always influenced the territorial government and were eager to separate so as to ensure their continued dominance. Alabama became a separate territory when Mississippi ratified the U.S. Constitution, and on December 14, 1819, it joined the Union as the twenty-second state.

Rosa Parks getting fingerprinted

Stride Toward Freedom | The battle for equal civil rights for African-Americans was largely staged within Alabama's boundaries. Following the Civil War and Reconstruction, the state's democratic government quickly reasserted its dominance over the state's black population by imposing the "Jim Crow" laws that segregated blacks from whites.

However, beginning in the 1950s, Alabama's black community started to resist. After seamstress Rosa Parks was arrested on December 1, 1955, for refusing to give up her seat on a bus to a white passenger, virtually the entire African-American community in Montgomery boycotted the city's bus system. At the outset of the boycott, twenty-six-year-old Martin Luther King, Jr., told an audience of more than ten thousand, "There comes a time when people get tired of being trampled over by the iron feet of oppression. We are not wrong in what we are doing. If we are wrong. . . justice is a lie." Eleven months later, the federal courts overturned Alabama's bus segregation laws, and King's espousal of peaceful protest to confront racial segregation began a new movement in American history.

MAINE

THE PINE TREE STATE

March 15, 1820

Capital: Augusta	**Area:** 30,865 square miles	**Motto:** I Direct
Bird: Chickadee	**Tree:** Eastern white pine	**Flower:** White pine cone and tassel

Maine Land | The first recorded European visits to Maine were made by John and Sebastian Cabot of England in 1497. When Italian navigator Giovanni da Verrazano claimed the land for France in 1524, he set the stage for a power struggle between the French and the English that would color the early part of America's history.

Both countries attempted to settle the region in the seventeenth century—the French at St. Croix Island in 1604, and the English at Popham Colony in 1607—and both settlements failed as a result of

Clipper ship

Maine's harsh winters. In 1622, King James I of England granted Sir Ferdinando Gorges a patent for a charter company in New England that gave him rights to much of the land as well as fishing rights in the region. Gorges divided the land holdings with his partner, John Mason, in 1629—Mason named his portion New Hampshire, and Gorges named his Maine, short for "mainland."

Did You Know?
The coastal town of Lubec is the easternmost place in the continental United States and the first place in America to see the sun rise each day.

Statehood | During the Revolutionary War, it became clear that Massachusetts was either unwilling or unable to protect its province of Maine against the British. Discontented Mainers argued that Massachusetts preferred absentee landlords to people actually living on the land, and a movement for statehood gained force. The British occupied Maine once again during the War of 1812, resulting in serious support of statehood.

Massachusetts finally agreed to the separation, and a state constitution was drawn up at a convention in Portland. Maine was the twenty-third state admitted to the Union on March 15, 1820, as part of the Missouri Compromise. Maine entered as a free state to balance Missouri's admission as a slave state.

Ship Shape | The tradition of shipbuilding in Maine has been around for nearly four hundred years. In fact, the first ship in America, the *Virginia*, was constructed in the Popham Colony in 1607. Forests cover almost ninety percent of Maine, and lumber for building ships has always been in ample supply.

From the late-eighteenth century through the early-twentieth century, Maine traded in rum, grain, and ice. Such precious and perishable cargo needed to be transported in fast ships. Maine clipper ships, which got their name because they moved so quickly they "clipped off" miles, sailed as far as China to trade. By the 1880s, a significant portion of Maine's population was working in the many shipyards along the coast.

MISSOURI

August 10, 1821

Capital: Jefferson City	Area: 69,675 square miles
Motto: The Welfare of the People Shall Be the Supreme Law	
Bird: Eastern bluebird	Tree: Flowering dogwood	Flower: White hawthorn blossom

Fur Galore | The French were the first Europeans to reach Missouri. The word Missouri is an Algonquin name for the people who lived near the mouth of the Missouri River. Explorers Jacques Marquette and Louis Jolliet discovered the Missouri River in 1673. René-Robert Cavelier, Sieur de La Salle, claimed the Missouri Valley for France in 1682. And French trappers, traders, and missionaries were the first to settle the region in the early part of the eighteenth century. The first permanent settlement was established at Sainte Genevieve in 1750.

Statehood | In 1817, Missourians were petitioning for entrance to the Union and their request spurred a major debate over the divisive issue of slavery. A solution, known as the Missouri Compromise, was finally worked out in 1820. The legislation allowed Missouri to enter the federal Union as a slave state, Maine to be admitted as a free state, and the Louisiana Territory to allow slavery in its southern half.

> **Did You Know?**
> The Gateway Arch in St. Louis, standing six hundred thirty feet tall, commemorates the city's central role as the "Gateway to the West" during the nineteenth century.

But the Missouri constitution, which allowed the practice of slavery and prohibited free blacks from entering the state, further troubled Congress as the U.S. Constitution stipulated that a person's rights must be equal in all the states. Missouri was finally admitted to the federal Union as the twenty-fourth state on August 10, 1821, after the state legislature

Gateway Arch

promised that the ban on free blacks would never be enforced—a promise that only lasted four years.

Scott Free? | Missouri was involved in much of the contentious slavery legislation that intensified the proslavery–antislavery tug-of-war prior to the Civil War—the critical Dred Scott case of 1857, a prime example. Dred Scott was a Missouri slave whose owner had taken him from Missouri to Minnesota, where slavery was banned. Scott sued for his freedom upon returning to Missouri on the grounds that residence in a free state constituted release from slavery. The case went all the way to the U.S. Supreme Court, which ultimately ruled that not only was Dred Scott not free, but also that the U.S. Constitution did not give Congress the authority to prohibit slavery in any of the territories. The ruling was a major blow to the abolitionist movement.

ARKANSAS

THE NATURAL STATE

June 15, 1836

Capital: Little Rock	Area: 53,225 square miles	Motto: The People Rule
Bird: Mockingbird	Tree: Pine	Flower: Apple Blossom

Slow to Grow | The Spaniard Hernando de Soto was the first European to lead an expedition through Arkansas on his quest for gold in 1541. Finding none, the Spanish abandoned activity in the region, and it remained unexplored for more than one hundred thirty years. The French then claimed the land, and Henri De Tonti (nicknamed "The Father of Arkansas") established the first permanent settlement, Arkansas Post, in 1686, with six residents.

Development of the region was sluggish throughout the ensuing century. When the entire Louisiana Territory was ceded to Spain in 1762, free land without taxes was offered as an incentive to prospective Spanish settlers. However, settlement of Arkansas continued to progress slowly. By the time the United States acquired the territory in 1803 as part of the Louisiana Purchase, there were fewer than four hundred settlers in Arkansas.

You Say ARkan-SAW, I Say Ar-KANSAS | When the French first explored Arkansas in the seventeenth century, the Native American Quapaw tribe inhabited the region west of the Mississippi River and north of the Arkansas River. Also known as the "downstream people," their Algonquian-speaking neighbors to the north called them the Arkansas, or "south wind." In the journals and maps of the explorers who visited the region throughout the early years of discovery, the name went through a variety of incarnations.

Père Marquette and Louis Jolliet spelled it AKANSEA in their

James Fulbright

Did You Know?
The Fulbright Scholarship Fund, used to pay for student studies abroad, is named for Arkansas Senator James Fulbright; he created the fund in 1946 using revenues from surplus World War II military equipment.

journal in 1673. A few years later, René-Robert Cavelier, Sieur de La Salle, wrote ACANSA on his map that charted the Mississippi River. Another map, drafted by Bénard de la Harpe between 1718 and 1722, called the Native Americans LES AKANSAS and the river ARKANSAS. When American explorer Zebulon Pike came along in 1811, he spelled the name of the region ARKANSAW. It was not until after Arkansas became a state that a final decision on the name was made that recognizes both its French and Native American roots: In 1881, a resolution was passed, declaring the spelling to be "Arkansas," but the pronunciation to be "Arkansaw."

Statehood | In 1819, the Arkansas Territory was separated from the Territory of Missouri. Settlement was hindered for a time because the federal government had relocated the Cherokee and Choctaw nations to western Arkansas, causing friction between the Native Americans and the white settlers. By 1828, both tribes had relinquished their lands in exchange for new areas in the west, and settlement proceeded at full tilt. Motivated by the population explosion of the 1830s, Arkansas petitioned for admission to the federal Union, becoming the twenty-fifth state on June 15, 1836.

MICHIGAN

THE WOLVERINE STATE

January 26, 1837

Capital: Lansing	Area: 56,809 square miles
Motto: If You Seek a Pleasant Penninsula, Look About You	
Bird: American robin	Tree: White pine	Flower: Apple blossom

Great Lake | In search of a river leading to the Pacific Ocean, French explorer Étienne Brûlé reached Michigan in 1618. Père Jacques Marquette founded a mission at Sault Sainte Marie in 1668, which became the first permanent settlement in the area. When the region was officially claimed for France under the sovereignty of King Louis XIV, more forts and missions were constructed around Michigan.

But in 1696, the French king ordered everyone out but the missionaries so as to concentrate efforts in settling the area along the Saint Lawrence River. With the French presence largely reduced, the British began encroaching on the land to take advantage of lucrative fur-trading opportunities. Michigan takes its name from the Algonquin term *michigama*, meaning "great lake."

Statehood | Having attained the minimum population required for statehood, Michigan applied to Congress for admission to the federal Union in 1834. However, a boundary dispute over a strip of land around present-day Toledo, Ohio, escalated into skirmishes between the militias of Ohio and Michigan. Because of this disagreement, Congress would not grant Michigan's request for statehood.

The territorial legislature balked at this refusal, saying it was not

Did You Know?
Michigan lays claim to the only floating post office in the world. The *J.W. Westcott II* is the only boat that delivers mail to ships at sea and has been operating for 125 years.

within its rights to block admission on these grounds and adopted a state constitution. A compromise, however, was soon reached: Congress gave the Toledo area to Ohio and compensated Michigan with a large stretch of land south of Lake Superior. Michigan became the twenty-sixth state on January 26, 1837.

War Heroes and a Heroine | Michiganers adopted the abolitionist cause with fervor. Fugitive slaves en route to freedom in Canada often made Michigan their last stop in the United States on the Underground Railroad. When the Civil War erupted in 1861, the state sent more than ninety thousand men, and one woman, to fight in the Union Army.

Sarah Emma Edmonds disguised herself as a man and fought alongside the men. Her identity was not discovered until she was wounded in battle. But Michigan's most famous soldier was Monroe resident, George Armstrong Custer. He fought bravely in the first Battle of Bull Run, the Battle of Gettysburg, and in most of the battles of Ulysses S. Grant's final campaign.

Wolverines

FLORIDA

March 3, 1845

Capital: Tallahassee	Area: 53,997 square miles	Motto: In God We Trust
Bird: Mockingbird	Tree: Sabal palmetto palm	Flower: Orange blossom

Fountain of Youth | Although slavers from Hispaniola may have preceded him, Spanish explorer Juan Ponce de León is credited with being the first European to set foot in Florida in 1513. Impressed by the wide variety of colorful flowers he spotted at Easter time, called *Pascua Florida* in Spanish, he named the region *La Florida*, meaning "Land of the Flowers." Returning to the Gulf Coast in 1521 with two ships full of colonists, Ponce de León was mortally wounded in a Native American attack. After his death, a dubious legend grew up around his explorations of Florida that claimed he had been on a quest for a magic fountain of youth.

> **Did You Know?**
>
> The *Sunshine State* produces more oranges—forty billion a year—than any other state. It also grows the most grapefruit, tangerines, limes, sugarcane, and watermelons.

Pedro Menéndez de Avilés, the Spanish governor of La Florida, established the first permanent settlement on the site of Saint Augustine in 1565. Named San Augustín, it was also the first permanent European settlement in all of America.

Statehood | Spain formally ceded Florida to the United States in 1821 after a long period of negotiations. Concerned that rebellion in their South American colonies would demand their full attention and military resources, the Spanish could not afford to go to war with the United States. Secretary of State John Quincy Adams was instrumental in enacting the Adams-Onís Treaty, in which the United States agreed to pay up

Buzz Aldrin on the moon

to five million dollars for land claims. On March 3, 1845, Florida joined the federal Union as the twenty-seventh state.

The Final Frontier | Cape Canaveral is home to the U.S. National Aeronautics and Space Administration's (NASA) Kennedy Space Center and the site of the groundbreaking Apollo 11 launch. On July 16, 1969, the spacecraft lifted off with the objective of bringing human beings safely to the moon and back. Four days later, during their fourteenth orbit of the moon, astronauts Neil Armstrong and Buzz Aldrin boarded the lunar module, Eagle, and descended toward the Sea of Tranquility.

After touching down softly on the lunar surface, Armstrong became the first human being to set foot on the moon, pronouncing the words: "That's one small step for a man, one giant leap for mankind." Armstrong and Aldrin worked for two and a half hours, collecting rock and core samples, and setting up various experiments on the lunar surface. They rejoined the rest of the Apollo 11 crew and returned to Earth on July 24.

TEXAS

THE LONE STAR STATE

December 29, 1845

| Capital: Austin | Area: 261,914 square miles | Motto: Friendship |
| Bird: Mockingbird | Tree: Pecan | Flower: Bluebonnet |

Shipwrecked | In 1528, Álvar Núñez Cabeza de Vaca and other members of a Spanish expedition were shipwrecked on the coast of Texas. He and three fellow survivors wandered through the vast Texan land, enduring many hardships, until they came upon a Spanish village in Mexico, from which a second expedition led by Francisco Vásquez de Coronado was dispatched.

After these initial expeditions, Spain gave up on the region until the French presence led them to restake their initial claim. Frenchman René-Robert Cavelier, Sieur de La Salle, established Fort Saint Louis near Matagorda Bay in 1685, where he was later killed in a Native

The Alamo

American attack. The Spanish eventually began setting up a series of missions in Texas to reinforce their domination of the area.

"Remember the Alamo" | A Franciscan mission in San Antonio, Texas, the Alamo retains a place in the nation's memory as the site of one of the most courageous defenses of independence ever staged. In 1836, a Mexican force of close to two thousand men launched an attack on a Texan garrison outside of San Antonio. With only one-tenth the number of men in his garrison, Colonel William Barrett Travis led the Texan force to the Alamo. There were fifteen civilians inside the mission at the time.

> **Did You Know?**
> The name Texas is derived from *tejas*, the Native American word for "friends" or "allies."

Mexican troops arrived and launched a major attack, bombarding the mission with heavy artillery. When they finally succeeded in breaking through the mission walls, the civilians were spared, but all of the Texan defenders were killed. Famous American frontiersman Davy Crockett was among them. Although they were defeated in the siege, the Texans managed to pick off six hundred Mexican soldiers. Under Sam Houston's command at the Battle in San Jacinto, Texans defeated Mexico while shouting the legendary battle cry, "Remember the Alamo!"

Statehood | The Republic of Texas was established in 1836, the second independent Republic in the United States after Vermont. The population was significant by that time, as settlers arrived en masse to take advantage of the free land offered as an incentive for settlement. The Republic lasted nine years before being annexed by the United States.

At first, the United States rejected the Texas treaty for annexation. But the federal government reconsidered the following year, and Texas became the twenty-eighth state in the federal Union on December 29, 1845. When the treaty was signed, Mexico immediately broke off its diplomatic relationship with the United States. The Mexican War erupted in 1846.

IOWA

THE HAWKEYE STATE

December 28, 1846

Capital: Des Moines	Area: 55,875 square miles	
Motto: Our Liberties We Prize, and Our Rights We Will Maintain		
Bird: Eastern goldfinch	Tree: Oak	Flower: Wild rose

Dubuque Mines | Reports of Iowa made in 1673 by French explorers Père Jacques Marquette and Louis Jolliet, the first-known Europeans to enter the region, praised its fertile, green lands. Iowa, named for the river and the Native American tribe that lived in the region, was claimed for France by René-Robert Cavelier, Sieur de La Salle, but only a few missionaries and fur traders passed through the area during French rule. The first settlement was not established until the Spanish were granted the land during the French and Indian War.

Julien Dubuque, the first white settler, was given leave to mine lead near present-day Dubuque in 1788. He hired members of the local Mesquaki tribe to work the mines and then sold the mined lead in St. Louis, Missouri. When Dubuque died in 1810, the Native Americans took possession of the land and continued mining. They dominated the region until white settlers began encroaching on Iowa in the early nineteenth century.

Statehood | Fewer than one hundred white settlers inhabited Iowa before 1832. When the area was organized as a territory in 1838, the white population rose rapidly. Small farmers arrived in droves to take advantage of the fertile land.

Iowans were not in support of joining the Union at first. They feared a strong federal government would not be in their best interests. Despite the support of the territorial governor, voters rejected two proposals for statehood. Finally, after some disagreement with Congress over state boundaries, Iowa became the twenty-ninth state of the Union on December 28, 1846.

Buffalo Bill Cody | Born in LeClaire in 1846, William F. "Buffalo Bill" Cody occupies center stage in America's image of the Wild West. He earned his nickname "Buffalo Bill" while working for the Kansas Pacific Railroad—in providing buffalo meat for the rail workers, he claimed to have killed more than four thousand buffalo in less than a year and a half. A rider for the Pony Express at age fourteen and a scout for the Union Army during the Civil War, Cody eventually became a showman, bringing the Wild West to the rest of the world.

Buffalo Bill was popularized by Ned Buntline's dime novels, which were inexpensive tales with exciting plots. After performing as himself in one of Buntline's dramas, he decided to create a show of his own using real cowboys and cowgirls as the performers. Wild Bill Hickock, Texas Jack, Annie Oakley, and Sitting Bull all performed at one time or another in his troupe. The traveling show (called "Buffalo Bill's Wild West") demonstrated bronco riding, roping, and other skills that helped shape the world's concept of the Wild West and did much to romanticize the American cowboy.

WISCONSIN

THE BADGER STATE

May 29, 1848

Capital: Madison	Area: 54,314 square miles	Motto: Forward
Bird: American robin	Tree: Sugar maple	Flower: Wood violet

Place of the Beaver | French explorer Jean Nicolet was the first European to arrive in Wisconsin. He reached Green Bay in 1634 while searching for the elusive Northwest Passage. The region was further explored by the French in the second half of the century, and the first missions were established by Jesuit priests near present-day Ashland and De Pere.

Initial exploration revealed the territory to be rich in fur-trapping opportunities. Trappers and traders came to Wisconsin to take advantage of the large population of beaver, whose pelts were in high demand in Europe. The name Wisconsin is a French derivation of the Ojibwa term for "place of the beaver," in reference to the Wisconsin River. The first trading post was established near present-day Green Bay in 1684. Aside from those in the fur-trading business, Wisconsin saw few white settlers until the nineteenth century.

Black Hawk War | The most drastic uprooting of Native American tribes occurred under the direction of President Andrew Jackson. In 1832, many of the Sac people who had been driven from their homeland in northwestern Illinois and relocated to a reservation in Iowa, returned to try and reclaim their land. Chief Black Hawk sent a peace emissary to negotiate the reappropriation of Sac land. Illinois settlers shot the representative, and what came to be known as the Black Hawk War ensued.

The Sac retreated through Wisconsin, trying to return to their reservation in Iowa. Black Hawk and his followers were closely pursued by local militia and army troops, and a number of battles were fought on Wisconsin soil. Before the Native Americans could cross the Bad Axe River, nearly all of them were killed in what came to be known as the Bad Axe Massacre. Many Wisconsin tribes relinquished titles to their lands east of the Mississippi in the following years, fearing a similar fate if they resisted.

Statehood | Wisconsin's population grew in spurts. The first wave arrived in the 1820s because of a mining boom; the second in the 1830s after Native American resistance was eliminated and the Erie Canal was completed; the third wave came from Europe (skilled miners from England, then a wave of northern Europeans) in the 1830s and 1840s.

The main impetus for statehood among Wisconsin residents was the need for federally funded internal improvements, such as roads, canals, and railroads. Voters felt that they would be able to secure more federal money as a state, and would also attract eastern money with the political strength and stability that statehood provided. Admission to the Union was endorsed in 1846, and the second draft of the state constitution was approved in 1848. On May 29, 1848, Wisconsin became the thirtieth state to enter the federal Union.

Chief Black Hawk

Did You Know?
Wisconsin received its nickname the *Badger State* because the miners who were among the first settlers in the region dug their homes out of the hillside or lived in the mine shafts—living underground as badgers do.

CALIFORNIA

September 9, 1850

Capital: Sacramento	Area: 155,973 square miles	Motto: I have found it
Bird: California valley quail	Tree: California redwood	Flower: Golden poppy

Paradise Island | Portuguese-born explorer Juão Rodrigues Cabrilho led the first European expedition (for Spain) into California in 1542. He sailed northward from Mexico, into the San Diego Bay and up the coast of California, claiming land for Spain along the way. The name California was given to the region by Cabrilho's expedition. California was a fictional island paradise described in a popular Spanish novel published in 1510. The beautiful landscape beheld by the explorers inspired the comparison.

James Marshall at Sutter's Mill

It was not until 1769 that any settlement activity took place in California. Gaspar de Portola and Junipero Serra set up a military post and a mission on behalf of the Spanish king at the site of present-day San Diego. By 1823, Franciscan missions had proliferated and formed a chain from San Diego to San Francisco.

Gold Rush | Right about the time that California was officially ceded to the United States in the Treaty of Guadalupe Hidalgo that formally ended the Mexican War (1846–1848), carpenter James Marshall discovered gold in the sawmill he was

> **Did You Know?**
> California claims both the largest and the oldest trees in the world—the General Sherman sequoia tree weighs 1,400 tons, and the bristlecone pine in Inyo National Forest is 4,600 years old.

building with his partner John Sutter northeast of Sacramento. Within a year of his discovery, the greatest gold rush in the history of the United States was underway. Ironically, Mexico sold California to the United States for fifteen million dollars the same year that gold—worth a total of one billion dollars—was discovered at Sutter's Mill.

In 1849, gold-hungry people, known as Forty-Niners, flocked to California from all over the world. By 1852 when the gold rush reached its peak, California's population had soared to two hundred twenty thousand. However, the gold rush ended quickly, and many prospectors either turned to farming or left the state.

Statehood | The deluge of settlers in California caused by the Gold Rush of 1849 created a strong need for an organized civil government. Congress was unable to establish a territory in the region because of the divisive issue of allowing slavery. But California residents took matters into their own hands; they held a convention in September 1849 and adopted a state constitution that prohibited slavery. The constitution was approved by popular vote, and the first legislature met to organize a state government. California was admitted to the federal Union on September 9, 1850, making it the thirty-first state in the Union.

MINNESOTA

THE GOPHER STATE

May 11, 1858

Capital: St. Paul	**Area:** 79,617 square miles	**Motto:** The Star of the North
Bird: Common loon	**Tree:** Red pine	**Flower:** Lady's slipper

Cloudy Water | In the process of extending their profitable fur trade beyond the Great Lakes region, French explorers were the first to claim Minnesota in the latter half of the seventeenth century. Father Louis Hennepin, a French priest sent to explore the northern part of the Mississippi River in 1680, discovered and named the Falls of Saint Anthony, which later became the Twin Cities of Saint Paul and Minneapolis. His extensive writings on the region sparked much French interest in the territory, mostly among fur traders.

> **Did You Know?**
> The "Land of 10,000 Lakes" actually has more than 15,000 lakes with 90,000 miles of shoreline—more than California, Hawaii, and Florida combined.

Pierre Gaultier de Varennes, Sieur de La Vérendrye, explored much of the Great Plains region in the United States and Canada in the hopes of locating the Northwest Passage. Although he failed to find the mythical waterway, he did claim much of the "Land of 10,000 Lakes" for France. The name Minnesota comes from the Sioux word for "cloudy water," which was how they described the Minnesota River.

Statehood | By 1863, Minnesota's Native American population had surrendered most of its land. When the Dakota treaties were approved in 1853, farmers rushed to the fertile valleys of the Mississippi and Minnesota Rivers. Over a period of four years, the population almost quadrupled, and the territorial legislature began lobbying for statehood.

A state constitutional convention was held in 1857; however, the Democratic and Republican delegations came to an impasse over the issue of slavery. The Republicans fiercely proclaimed it immoral, and the Democrats held an equally strong opinion that slaves were property. The two parties met separately, and each drew up a constitution. After a remarkably short period of deliberation, a compromise constitution was drawn up and approved in a popular election. Despite opposition from slave states in Congress, Minnesota was admitted to the Union as the thirty-second state on May 11, 1858.

Bunyan and Babe | According to legend, Paul Bunyan was a hero of the lumber camps in the American Northwest. A logger of unmatched strength, vision, and speed, he made his mark on the American landscape with the help of his giant blue ox, Babe. The story goes that, with Babe at his side, he created Puget Sound, the Grand Canyon, and the Black Hills, hauling entire forests at one time.

This "tall tale" circulated through the logging camps of Minnesota in the early twentieth century, changing as it went with each new telling. In 1910, some of the stories were collected, transcribed, and published in a series of pamphlets advertising the Red River Lumber Company. Minnesota has many proud testaments to the legendary Paul Bunyan: the giant roadside attraction in Akeley, the Paul Bunyan Trail from Brainerd to Hackensack, and his "grave" in Kelliher.

OREGON

THE BEAVER STATE

February 14, 1859

Capital: Salem	Area: 96,003 square miles	Motto: The Union
Bird: Western meadowlark	Tree: Douglas fir	Flower: Oregon grape

Land of Missed Opportunity | There were many missed opportunities to explore Oregon, which comes from the French *ouragan*, meaning "hurricane," in the early years of European presence in the New World. Spanish navigator Bartolome Ferrelo sailed up the Oregon coast in 1542, but did not explore the shores. British explorer Sir Francis Drake made it to the Oregon coast in 1579, but turned back because of thick fog. In 1778, British navigator James Cook also arrived in the Pacific Northwest while seeking the fictional Northwest Passage, but failed to explore Oregon.

The Oregon Trail

Finally, American fur trader Captain Robert Gray set foot on an Oregon shore in 1788 and discovered the mouth of the Columbia River, which he named after his boat. Meriwether Lewis and William Clark made further expeditions on the Columbia River in 1805. The New York fur trader John Jacob Astor established the first white settlement at Astoria in 1811.

Busy Beavers | The origins of Oregon's nickname, "The Beaver State," can be traced back to the early part of the nineteenth century. The fashion of the times in America's northeastern cities was to wear fur hats. When Oregon was first explored, fur traders were drawn to the region's rivers and streams, which were teeming with beavers. Fur companies soon vied for control of the trapping and trading industry in the area and sent "mountain men" to stake claims and establish trading posts.

When the beaver-hat craze had subsided and Oregon's beaver supply had dwindled, many of these mountain men became guides on the famous Oregon Trail. Propaganda in the East, coupled with an economic depression in the Midwest, brought huge numbers of pioneers across the trail to settle in Oregon.

Statehood | Between 1842 and 1843, one thousand pioneers crossed the Oregon Trail, and in 1848, President James K. Polk signed a bill to create the Oregon Territory, which incorporated the lands of present-day Oregon, Washington, Idaho, as well as parts of Montana and Wyoming.

Land ownership was a big issue during the early years of the territory. Congress passed the Oregon Donation Land Act of 1850, which established a prorated system of land grants that aided pioneers already cultivating the land and encouraged settlement. The population increase spurred the creation of a state constitution in 1857, and Oregon became the thirty-third state to enter the Union on February 14, 1859.

KANSAS

THE SUNFLOWER STATE

January 29, 1861

Capital: Topeka	**Area:** 81,823 square miles	**Motto:** To the Stars Through Difficulties
Bird: Western meadowlark	**Tree:** Cottonwood	**Flower:** Wild sunflower

People of the South Wind | Kansas, which takes its name from the Kansa tribe meaning "people of the south wind," was first explored by Francisco Vásquez de Coronado in 1541. He led an expedition from New Mexico in search of a kingdom called Quivira, rumored to be a place of great wealth. Coronado instead found a village of Wichita people in present-day Kansas. He returned to New Mexico a month later, and the Spanish largely ignored the region for more than one hundred fifty years.

> **Did You Know?**
> Born in Atchison, Amelia Earhart was the first woman to be granted a pilot's license and the first woman to complete a solo flight across the Atlantic Ocean.

The French moved into Kansas during this time and conducted a prosperous fur trade. The land changed hands many times over the course of the eighteenth century until it was granted to the United States as part of the Louisiana Purchase in 1803. The Lewis and Clark Expedition explored the area near the junction of the Kansas and Missouri Rivers in 1804, and Zebulon Pike traveled overland through the Great Plains in 1806, which he reported to be largely uninhabitable.

Statehood | The Kansas Territory, established in 1854 as part of the Kansas-Nebraska Act, was divided by a proslavery–antislavery tug-of-war throughout its territorial years. In 1857, the Free State Party gained control of the legislature, but settlers in favor of slavery continued to press for admission to the Union as a slave state. Both sides drew up constitu-

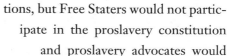

tions, but Free Staters would not participate in the proslavery constitution and proslavery advocates would not participate in the Free State constitution.

Ultimately, both constitutions were rejected by Congress. In 1859, a new constitution was proposed that included an article prohibiting slavery. Kansas voters approved it by a two-to-one margin. On January 29, 1861, Kansas was granted admission to the Union as the thirty-fourth state.

With All Deliberate Speed | Dwight D. Eisenhower grew up in Abilene, Kansas, and went on to become one of our nation's more popular and pragmatic presidents. He appointed Earl Warren to the position of chief justice of the Supreme Court in 1953, and in so doing ushered in a new era of judicial history that greatly expanded the civil rights and civil liberties of the American people. The benchmark case of the Warren Court was Brown v. Topeka Board of Education.

On May 17, 1954, the Supreme Court unanimously decided that the separation of educational facilities for white students and black students violated the Fourteenth Amendment of the U.S. Constitution, which guarantees all citizens "equal protection of the laws." The Court ruled that segregation in public schools made them inherently unequal, and therefore, unconstitutional. The following year, the Warren Court ordered the states to desegregate schools "with all deliberate speed" and marked a major victory for the Civil Rights Movement.

WEST VIRGINIA

THE MOUNTAIN STATE

June 20, 1863

Capital: Charleston	Area: 24,087 square miles	Motto: Mountaineers Are Always Free
Bird: Cardinal	Tree: Sugar maple	Flower: Big rhododendron

Almost Heaven │ West Virginia formed part of Virginia until the second half of the nineteenth century. But the first-recorded European visit to the western portion of the state was made in 1669 by John Lederer, a German physician sent by Virginia's governor to explore the region beyond the majestic Blue Ridge Mountains. Explorers and fur traders were soon to follow. By 1830, Virginia began granting tracts of its western land to pioneers, who were predominantly German and Scots–Irish immigrants in search of religious tolerance and free land.

John Brown's uprising

John Brown's Body | John Brown, regarded by fellow abolitionists as a martyr to the cause of human freedom, dedicated most of his life to the education of young blacks and made many attempts to end slavery by force. Supported by abolitionists in the northeastern states, Brown planned to establish a free and independent state in the Blue Ridge Mountains to serve as a safe haven for runaway slaves. On October 16, 1859, he and a small group of men seized the U.S. arsenal and armory at Harper's Ferry and took control of the town.

John Brown was forced to surrender when local militia and a company of U.S. Marines surrounded them. He was arrested and charged with treason and murder. Although Brown distinguished himself with an eloquent defense in trial, he was convicted and hanged in Charles Town.

Statehood | Proposals for a separate western state had been made in Virginia as early as 1820. While eastern Virginia had mostly large tobacco plantations worked by slaves, West Virginia was peopled by immigrants and hardworking frontiersmen with small farms. Western Virginians resented the political domination by eastern planters and complained of being overtaxed and underrepresented in the state legislature. When Virginia seceded from the Union in 1861, western Virginians set a plan in motion to create their own state.

> **Did You Know?**
> Grave Creek Mound in Moundsville, West Virginia, is the tallest Native American burial mound in the world, standing sixty-nine feet tall.

It is written into the U.S. Constitution that the division of a state cannot take place without its own consent. So delegates from the western counties declared the offices of the state government in Richmond to be empty and established the Reformed Government of Virginia in Wheeling. President Abraham Lincoln then recognized Wheeling as the seat of the legal government of Virginia. In October of 1861, elected delegates drafted a constitution modeled on those of the Northern states, and on June 20, 1863, West Virginia became the thirty-fifth state to join the federal Union.

NEVADA

THE SILVER STATE

October 31, 1864

Capital: Carson City	**Area:** 109,806 square miles	**Motto:** All for Our Country
Bird: Mountain bluebird	**Tree:** Single-leaf piñon	**Flower:** Sagebrush

The Great Basin | Although the Spanish claimed Nevada (the Spanish word for "snow covered") early on, they founded no settlements in the region. Fur trappers, Peter Skene Ogden and Jedediah Smith, were the first to explore Nevada in the 1820s. Ogden discovered the Humboldt River and the Humboldt Sink in 1828. Smith was the first white man to cross Nevada in 1826, exploring much of what John Charles Frémont later dubbed the Great Basin.

The Silver Lining | Mining booms following the discovery of gold and silver in Nevada contributed to much of the state's early history. When the Comstock Lode, a metal-yielding vein near Carson City, was uncovered in 1859, a flood of immigrants came to work in the mines. The lode produced more than three hundred million dollars in gold and silver during its first twenty years of operation.

> **Did You Know?**
> The Hoover Dam, completed in 1936, contains as much steel as the Empire State Building and enough concrete to pave a cross-country two-lane highway.

The U.S. Mint opened a branch in Carson City in 1863. With the mines so close by, it was the perfect location to mint silver dollars and other coins. However, the Coinage Act of 1873, nick-named the "Crime of '73" by supporters of silver money, ended the minting of silver dollars and contributed to a dramatic drop in the price of silver. The Carson City mint branch remained open until 1893, when rail transportation made the satellite branch unnecessary.

Statehood | The Territory of Nevada was created in 1861, and shortly thereafter, a public referendum revealed overwhelming support for statehood. Delegates met at a constitutional convention in 1863 and drafted a state constitution. The powerful San Francisco mining corporations, which owned many of the mines in Nevada, urged ratification as they felt their interests would be better served by elected judges rather than territorial judges. Small mine owners and workers opposed the constitution, and in 1864, it was rejected by popular vote.

Congress and the Lincoln administration, however, favored Nevada statehood as they were trying to gain support for the Thirteenth Amendment to the U.S. Constitution, which outlawed slavery. Congress passed the Nevada Enabling Act, and a second constitution was drafted. It established that mine proceeds, not property, would be taxed, which appeased small mine owners and ensured ratification. Nevada became the thirty-sixth state in the Union on October 31, 1864.

Comstock Lode

NEBRASKA

THE CORNHUSKER STATE

March 1, 1867

Capital: Lincoln	**Area:** 76,878 square miles	**Motto:** Equality Before the Law
Bird: Western meadowlark	**Tree:** Cottonwood	**Flower:** Goldenrod

Flat Water | Although the Spanish and the French both made sweeping claims of western lands in the sixteenth and seventeenth centuries, the first-recorded exploration of Nebraska was made by French adventurer Étienne Veniard de Bourgmont in 1714. He traveled as far north as the Platte River. The Oto named the Platte River *Nebrathka*, meaning "flat water," and the name Nebraska was eventually given to the land. French and Spanish activity continued in the area until the Louisiana Purchase of 1803.

The first permanent settlement in Nebraska was built at Bellevue in 1823, and became a center for fur trade and missionary activities. However, reports by explorer Stephen H. Long of a vast desert in the Great Plains region, deterred further settlement for some time. The U.S. government utilized the site for the relocation of Native American tribes.

Homestead Laws | To encourage settlement of the West, Congress enacted a series of incentive measures called the Homestead Laws that allowed settlers without capital to acquire land. Plans for such legislation were afoot early on; however, Southerners feared that homesteaders would be against the practice of slavery and voted against the laws. Only when the Southern states seceded from the Union did the Homestead Laws pass.

The first Homestead farm was established in 1862 near Beatrice, Nebraska. In order to acquire land under the act, a citizen had to be at least twenty-one years old or the head of a family or have served actively in the U.S. Armed Services for at least two weeks. Each homesteader could be granted up to one hundred sixty acres, and he would earn the title to the land after the tract had been settled or cultivated for five years. Along with railroad land grants, the Homestead Laws transferred two-thirds of Nebraska's public lands to white settlers.

Statehood | Nebraska became a separate territory with the passing of the Kansas-Nebraska Act in 1854. While violence quickly broke out over the issue of whether to permit slavery in the Kansas Territory, Nebraskans, more concerned with settling the land, had little interest in supporting the institution. President Lincoln recognized Nebraska as an asset to the Union struggle during the Civil War. Congress passed an act in 1864 that would enable the territory to draft a state constitution and apply for statehood.

Nebraskans were divided on the issue of statehood—opponents, mostly Democrats, felt that the cost of a state government would offset the benefits. Although voters rejected plans to petition for statehood in 1864, they narrowly approved a constitution two years later. President Andrew Johnson, Democratic president appointed after Lincoln's assassination, vetoed Nebraska's application for statehood, saying that it violated the U.S. Constitution. But Congress overruled his veto and admitted Nebraska to the Union on March 1, 1867, making it the thirty-seventh state to join.

COLORADO

THE CENTENNIAL STATE

August 1, 1876

Capital: Denver	Area: 103,730 square miles	Motto: Nothing without Providence
Bird: Lark bunting	Tree: Colorado blue spruce	Flower: Rocky Mountain columbine

Colored Red | The Spanish were the first Europeans to arrive in Colorado, formally claiming the land in the early eighteenth century. Colorado means "colored red" in Spanish; the name was first given to the river because of the red soil that gives the river its color. And although René-Robert Cavelier, Sieur de La Salle, claimed the entire area between the Allegheny Mountains and the Rocky Mountains for France in 1682, he never actually ventured west of the Mississippi. Zebulon Pike was the first American to lead an expedition into the region in 1806.

"Pikes Peak or Bust" | In 1858, gold was discovered in the Pikes Peak region of the eastern Rocky Mountains. Within a year, nearly one hundred thousand gold-hungry prospectors poured into Colorado from the eastern states, using "Pikes Peak or Bust" as their slogan. Mining camps and boomtowns sprung up around the area. Colorado was still part of the Kansas Territory at the time, and with all of the activity in the region due to the gold rush, settlers felt a strong need for their own territorial government.

> **Did You Know?**
> While standing atop Pikes Peak in 1893, Katherine Lee Bates was inspired to write the poem "America the Beautiful," as she admired the "amber waves of grain" in the wheat fields on the high plains.

In 1859, a constitution was drawn up for the Jefferson Territory (as it was called at the time), and a governor and legislature were elected. The new legislature met to discuss taxes, mining rights, land titles, and other important frontier topics, then sent delegates to Congress to lobby for

Prospector en route to Pikes Peak

independent territorial status. However, Congress was preoccupied with mounting tensions between North and South, and it was not until 1861, that the unofficial Jefferson Territory officially became the Colorado Territory.

Statehood | Thousands of people flocked to Colorado when gold was discovered in 1859. But most left the mountains when the rush was over, leaving a small population behind. Remaining residents began a movement for statehood; however, the first state constitution proposed in Colorado was rejected by popular vote.

Attempts at statehood were largely ignored in Congress because of the heated debate between the Republicans and Democratic President Andrew Johnson over treatment of the defeated Southern states after the Civil War. Johnson vetoed statehood with the rationale that the population was too small; however, Congress approved the bill in 1875. Colorado delegates proposed a state constitution a year later that was approved by a three-to-one margin, and on August 1, 1876, Colorado joined the Union as the thirty-eighth state.

NORTH DAKOTA

November 2, 1889

Capital: Bismarck	Area: 68,994 square miles	
Motto: Liberty and Union Now and Forever, One and Inseparable		
Bird: Western meadowlark	Tree: American elm	Flower: Wild prairie rose

Seeking Northwest Passage | Réne-Robert Cavelier, Sieur de La Salle, claimed North Dakota for the French in 1682. The name Dakota means "friends" or "allies" and is another name for the Sioux people, who inhabited the region before the Europeans arrived. The French king later authorized Pierre Gaultier de Varennes, Sieur de La Vérendrye, to explore the land in search of lucrative fur-trading opportunities as well as

Theodore Roosevelt

a route that supposedly connected the Atlantic Ocean to the Pacific Ocean—the so-called Northwest Passage.

Hunting Trips of a Ranch Man | The grasslands of western North Dakota, perfect for fattening cattle quickly, attracted cattle ranchers from far and wide once the railroad arrived. One such rancher was future U.S. President Theodore Roosevelt. At the age of twenty-five, he traveled to the Dakota Territory to hunt in the Badlands and soon established the Elkhorn and Maltese Cross ranches on the Little Missouri River.

During his time as a rancher, Theodore Roosevelt raised five thousand head of cattle, chaired the Stockgrowers' Association, and wrote books on a variety of subjects—from *Hunting Trips of a Ranch Man* to *The Winning of the West*. When he refocused his energies on politics, he exhibited the same gusto that characterized his early years as a rancher. A champion of public interest, Theodore Roosevelt made domestic and economic reforms that attacked the problems posed by modern industrial society on a national scale.

Did You Know?
The town of Rugby is the geographical center of North America—a rock obelisk with a Canadian and American flag on either side stands on the location.

Statehood | The Dakota Territory, which was comprised of North and South Dakota, as well as large portions of Montana and Wyoming, was established in 1861. Although the Homestead Act offered enticing incentives, it was not until the railroads arrived in the 1870s and 1880s that rapid settlement and agriculture caught on.

In 1883, the influential railroad lobbyist Alexander McKenzie arranged to have the territorial capital moved from Yankton, in the south, to Bismarck, in the north. A general election in 1887 established the boundaries of the northern and southern Dakota Territory, and two years later, Congress authorized both Dakotas, Montana, and Washington to become states. On November 2, 1889, North Dakota became the thirty-ninth state of the Union.

SOUTH DAKOTA

THE MOUNT RUSHMORE STATE

November 2, 1889

Capital: Pierre	**Area:** 75,898 square miles	**Motto:** Under God the People Rule
Bird: Ring-necked pheasant	**Tree:** Black Hills spruce	**Flower:** Pasque flower

Pierre | French explorers and fur traders crossed into South Dakota in the middle of the eighteenth century. The region was absorbed into the upper portion of the Louisiana Territory at the turn of the century and then ceded to Spain in 1762. France regained the land in 1800 and then granted it to the United States three years later as part of the Louisiana Purchase.

Meriwether Lewis and William Clark's reports of numerous fur-bearing animals in the territory brought many fur-trading companies to South Dakota. A regional manager of one of these fur companies, Pierre Chuteau, Jr., dominated commercial activities in the fur trade for close to thirty years and his first name was given as the name of the state capital, Pierre, pronounced "peer."

Did You Know?
Sculptor Gutzon Borglum, who studied under Auguste Rodin, was the artist behind the creation of Mount Rushmore. Each figure is sixty feet high with a nose measuring about twenty feet high, a mouth measuring eighteen feet in length, with each eye measuring eleven feet across.

Wounded Knee | In the late nineteenth century, a new religious movement began among the Sioux called the ghost dance, which called for the disappearance of the white people and the return of the buffalo. Fearing rebellion, the local white settlers banned the ghost dance and withheld monies owed the Sioux by the government.

In 1890, the U.S. government tried to arrest the Sioux leader Sitting Bull on a reservation in North Dakota to prohibit him from leading a revolt. A scuffle ensued and Sitting Bull was killed along with twelve

Mount Rushmore

other Sioux. The rest of his followers fled with the U.S. Army in hot pursuit. A group of them were tracked to an encampment near Wounded Knee Creek in South Dakota, where the U.S. Army killed nearly 370 members of the Sioux tribe.

Statehood | Railroad construction increased in the southern Dakota Territory in the late 1870s, attracting settlers and bolstering the economy. This population boom inspired a movement for statehood, and when Alexander McKenzie had the capital moved to the northern Dakota Territory in 1883, a campaign to establish a separate southern state began in earnest. Opposing the admission of two Republican states out of the Dakota Territory, Democrats in Congress and Democratic President Grover Cleveland blocked South Dakota's petition for statehood. Their path was not cleared until Republicans gained control of the presidency and of both houses in Congress in 1888. South Dakota entered the Union on November 2, 1889 as the fortieth state.

MONTANA

THE TREASURE STATE

November 8, 1889

Capital: Helena	Area: 145,556 square miles	Motto: Gold and Silver
Bird: Western meadowlark	Tree: Ponderosa pine	Flower: Bitterroot

Shining Mountains | Although adventurous French fur traders may have reached Montana in the middle of the eighteenth century, the area was not formally explored for some time. The land west of the Mississippi was a major point of contention for the French and the English before the outbreak of the French and Indian War in 1754. When the French began to lose the war, they asked for Spain's alliance in return for land, which included Montana, the Spanish word for "mountainous."

Under Napoleon's rule thirty-eight years later, France reclaimed the land and sold it to the United States in the Louisiana Purchase of 1803. Shortly thereafter, President Thomas Jefferson sent Lewis and Clark on their famous expedition from St. Louis, Missouri, to explore Montana and the other newly acquired lands.

Little Bighorn | When gold was discovered in Montana in the 1860s, white prospectors poured into the area and continually encroached on Native American land. The Sioux were incensed by the settlers using the

> **Did You Know?**
> The Elk, deer, and antelope populations in Montana outnumber the human population.

Bozeman Trail, which cut across Sioux territory in the Great Plains, and frequently attacked settlements and travelers along the path. In 1868, the government negotiated a treaty with the Sioux that granted them a reservation in the Black Hills.

Unhappy with the agreement, Sioux leaders Sitting Bull and Crazy Horse remained by the Bozeman Trail with members of their tribe. The U.S. government decided to take action against the Native American threat in 1876 and sent troops in to forcibly move the group to the reservation. General George Custer headed up the regiment that fought the Sioux at the Battle of Little Bighorn. Grossly outnumbered, the soldiers suffered a crushing defeat, and General Custer was killed in the battle. More reinforcements were eventually sent in by the U.S. government; Crazy Horse surrendered in 1877 and Sitting Bull in 1881.

Statehood | The population growth of the early 1860s in Montana created the need for a more centralized form of government. In 1864, the Montana Territory was established with a popularly elected bicameral legislature. A petition was made to Congress after the first constitutional convention in 1866, but Montana's population was still too small to be considered for statehood. Congress refused the territory's second bid for statehood in 1884, but approved the state constitution drawn up at the third convention in 1889, that limited the power of the governor and gave rural communities a high level of representation to counterbalance the forceful mining lobby. On November 8, 1889, Montana was finally admitted to the Union as the forty-first state.

Sitting Bull

WASHINGTON

Capital: Olympia	**Area:** 66,582 square miles	**Motto:** By and By
Bird: Willow goldfinch	**Tree:** Western hemlock	**Flower:** Western rhododendron

North Pacific | The Spanish claimed Washington for their king in 1775, and British explorer Captain James Cook charted the coast in 1778, claiming the land for England. These conflicting claims caused friction between the two countries. In an effort to avoid war, they agreed to respect one another's settlements and commercial activities.

The United States acquired Washington as part of the Louisiana Purchase in 1803, and Thomas Jefferson commissioned the Lewis and Clark expedition to explore the area. Their initial reports inspired fur-trading pioneers to settle the region. John Jacob Astor was the first American to establish a settlement in Washington.

Grand Dam | President Franklin Delano Roosevelt took office in 1932 and implemented the Public Works Administration (PWA) in an effort to combat the soaring unemployment rates caused by the Great Depression. Between 1933 and 1942, the PWA constructed the Grand Coulee Dam on the Columbia River, the largest dam ever built at the time. As part of Roosevelt's recovery program, folksinger Woody Guthrie wrote "Roll On, Columbia" about the construction of the monumental dam.

Did You Know?
Washington, the only state to be named for a U.S. president, has more glaciers than the other forty-seven contiguous states combined.

Statehood | The Columbia Territory (present-day Washington) was established on March 2, 1853. The territorial legislature petitioned for statehood in 1878, but a number of factors blocked their entrance to the Union: border disputes, insufficient population, and the Democratic majority in Congress. When Republicans gained control of Congress in 1888, they passed enabling acts that cleared the way for statehood. The Columbia Territory was renamed Washington when it became the forty-second state on November 11, 1889.

Grand Coulee Dam

IDAHO

THE GEM STATE

July 3, 1890

Capital: Boise	**Area:** 82,751 square miles	**Motto:** It Is Forever
Bird: Mountain bluebird	**Tree:** White pine	**Flower:** Syringa

Gem of the Mountains | Located in the remote mountains of the American northwest, Idaho was the last state to be seen and settled by white people. Its name was originally believed to be a Native American word meaning "gem of the mountains," though some hold that it was the invention of a white politician. With the help of their Shoshone guide Sacagawea, explorers Meriwether Lewis and William Clark discovered Idaho in 1805. Seeking a water route to the Pacific, the expedition attempted to cross the difficult Bitterroot Mountains with inadequate supplies. But the Nez Percé Indians came to their aid by providing them with food, offering them guidance for the trek, helping them find good timber for making canoes, and trading horses for goods.

Lewis and Clark with Sacagawea

Silver and Potatoes | In the late 1800s, the arrival of railroads in Idaho gave miners and farmers a conduit for their most successful yields: silver and potatoes. The concentration of silver in the Coeur d'Alene region produced two billion dollars of revenue in 1885, making it the largest lead–silver district in the country. Dangerous conditions in the mines, however, led to violent strikes that twice called for the imposition of martial law to restore order at the end of the nineteenth century.

In addition to the influx of miners following the discovery of silver, lead, and gold, Idaho also attracted farmers. As the soil and weather conditions of the region are similar to those of the Andes Mountains of South America where potatoes were first grown, it was an ideal place to cultivate the crop. Using dams and irrigation systems, farmers managed to convert more than two million acres of range lands into farms. Much of the early potato production in Idaho was used to feed miners.

> **Did You Know?**
> Hell's Canyon is the deepest gorge in the United States—it has a 7,900-foot drop from the canyon's ridge to the Snake River.

Statehood | Idaho's present boundaries were established after both Montana and Wyoming had become separate territories in 1868. Although the mountainous wilderness and arid plains of Idaho initially discouraged settlement, a number of factors contributed to its later desirability. The discovery of gold attracted hordes of miners, the abundant grazing lands brought cattle ranchers in abundance, the Idaho panhandle produced excellent grains and drew farmers to the region, and the new transportation links tied the rather isolated territory to the rest of the country.

A proposal to redivide the territory by attaching parts of Idaho to Washington and Nevada was approved by Congress in 1887, but the territorial governor's last-minute plea foiled the plan. Ultimately, the region's Republican majority swayed Congress' decision to grant Idaho admission to the Union on July 3, 1890, as the forty-third state.

WYOMING

Capital: Cheyenne	Area: 97,105 square miles	Motto: Equal Rights
Bird: Meadowlark	Tree: Cottonwood	Flower: Indian paintbrush

Upon the Great Plain | For a land that few people had ever set foot in, Wyoming (a derivation of the Delaware Indian word meaning "upon the great plain") was often discussed at the territorial bargaining table. It was included in three major land transactions, the Louisiana Purchase (1803), the establishment of the Oregon Territory (1848), and the Treaty of Guadalupe Hidalgo (1848). Although the Spanish and French may have passed through the region sometime between the sixteenth and eighteenth centuries, John Colter of the Lewis and Clark expedition was the first-known white explorer to have visited Wyoming in 1807.

Women's Suffrage | Although Wyoming had a rather rough-and-tumble image as the *Cowboy State*, it was also one of the most politically progressive states in the early days of statehood. Women were given the right to vote in 1869, hence the nickname the *Equality State*. In addition to suffrage rights, the first territorial legislature, composed entirely of Democrats, gave women the right to own property, the right to hold office, and the right to wages on par with men for jobs with similar requirements.

> **Did You Know?**
> Yellowstone National Park, including Old Faithful Geyser, the Grand Canyon of the Yellowstone, and Mammoth Hot Springs, became the world's first national park in 1872.

Legislators hoped to attract more female settlers to the area and to publicize Wyoming back East with this groundbreaking legislation. The first female justice of the peace, Esther Hobart Morris, was soon appointed, along with the first women jurors. Wyoming became the first state to elect a woman to statewide office and to the position of governor.

Statehood | Fewer than one thousand white settlers lived in Wyoming in the mid-1860s. However, the discovery of a rich gold deposit (the Carissa Lode), the construction of the transcontinental railroad, the abundance of coal mines, and a booming cattle industry brought thousands of people to the region. Despite the phenomenal population growth, the numbers were still rather low to be considered for statehood.

Nonetheless, the territorial legislature organized a constitutional convention in 1889 and a state constitution was drafted. Most of the articles were drawn from other state constitutions, except for the provision for control of all waterways within Wyoming and the unique grant of women's suffrage. Voters approved the constitution, and despite some objections from Congress on these more radical articles, Wyoming was admitted to the Union as the forty-fourth state on July 10, 1890.

Emigrants crossing the plains

UTAH

THE BEEHIVE STATE

January 4, 1896

Capital: Salt Lake City	Area: 82,168 square miles	Motto: Industry
Bird: Seagull	Tree: Blue spruce	Flower: Sego lily

Mountaintop Dwellers | Utah, which is a Native American word meaning "mountaintop dwellers," was explored by Juan Maria Antonio de Rivera, a Spaniard who traveled from New Mexico to Moab, Utah in 1765. He was the first-known European to visit the region, and was followed eleven years later by two Franciscan friars, who developed trade between the merchants of Santa Fe, New Mexico, and the Native Americans in Utah.

Fur trappers began arriving in the area from Canada, New Mexico, and Missouri during the 1820s. Jedediah Smith left the Great Salt Lake in 1826 and, crossing Utah, became the first American to reach California overland. Explorer John Charles Frémont made maps and scientific reports of the region twenty years later that inspired further settlement.

> **Did You Know?**
> Rainbow Bridge, the world's largest natural-rock span, is made of solid sandstone and stands 290 feet high and 275 feet wide.

Exodus | Mormonism, or The Church of Jesus Christ of Latter-day Saints, was founded in 1830 by Joseph Smith. Its principal doctrine holds that Christianity has been corrupted over time and restoration of the true Christian gospel must be sought through divine revelation. Although Mormons believe in the toleration of all religions, they see their church as the only one that is fully recognized by God. In the mid-nineteenth century, church followers in Ohio, Missouri, and Illinois were persecuted for their beliefs and practices, and they moved west in search of a place to settle away from the oppressive gentiles, or non-Mormons.

Under the leadership of Brigham Young, a party of Mormons crossed the Wasatch Range in 1847, and established the first permanent white settlement in Utah near the Great Salt Lake. Young's group was joined by more than one thousand Mormons, traveling by wagon train from western Iowa. They set about irrigating and planting the land, and by 1850, close to ten thousand Mormons had settled the region.

Statehood | When the Mexican War ended and ownership of Utah was transferred to the United States, Brigham Young called for a state constitution to be drawn up in 1849. Eager to maintain the independence of the Mormon colonies, he proposed a state called Deseret (meaning "honeybee" in the Book of Mormon) comprising all of the western states. Congress would not recognize the state of Deseret, but through the Compromise Measures of 1850, did create a separate Utah territory. By 1868, it was reduced to the state's present-day size.

Brigham Young

From the time Deseret was first proposed in 1849, Utahans consistently petitioned for statehood and Congress consistently refused them. The main reason for this refusal was the practice of polygamy among the Mormons. Congress passed a series of federal antibigamy laws and initiated an aggressive campaign to stamp the practice out altogether. Finally, in 1890, Mormon leaders advised the congregation to abstain from polygamy, thus clearing the way for statehood. A state constitution was drawn up in 1895 that not only outlawed polygamy, but gave women the right to vote. It was approved and Utah became the forty-fifth state in the Union on January 4, 1896.

OKLAHOMA

Capital: Oklahoma City	**Area:** 68,679 square miles	**Motto:** Labor Conquers All Things
Bird: Scissor-tailed flycatcher	**Tree:** Redbud	**Flower:** Mistletoe

Ohhh, Oklahoma | Spanish explorers crossed into Oklahoma in 1541 on their treasure hunt for the legendary Seven Cities of Cíbola. The French were the next to arrive, following the claims made by René-Robert Cavelier, Sieur de La Salle, in the 1680s. Eventually, fur traders arrived, military and trading posts were established, and settlements were made. It was not until after the French and Indian War and the Louisiana Purchase that Americans ventured into Oklahoma, which is a combination of Choctaw words meaning "red" and "people."

Trail of Tears

Five Civilized Tribes | The Choctaw, Chickasaw, Creek, Seminole, and Cherokee once inhabited most of the southeastern United States. Whites collectively referred to them as the Five Civilized Tribes because their organization and economy was based on the structure of European nations. Many had also adopted the ways of white agriculture, commerce, and politics.

Despite Native American efforts at assimilation, following the War of 1812, Southern members of Congress continually lobbied for their removal in order to open the rich lands up to white settlement. Eventually, the U.S. Government began negotiating removal treaties with the Five Civilized Tribes—each tribe was to give up their current land in exchange for annual payments of food and money as well as land in present-day Oklahoma. The Indian Territory was established in 1834 and the government set about forcibly uprooting and relocating the tribes to this allotted land along what came to be known as the Trail of Tears.

> **Did You Know?**
> The nickname the Sooner State stems from settlers who rushed to claim plots of land in the Indian Territory before the official start of the "land rush" in 1889.

Statehood | White settlement continued to encroach on Native American lands. Congress finally determined that before the Oklahoma Territory could become a state, it had to absorb the Indian Territory and all Native Americans had to become U.S. citizens. The federal Dawes Commission formed in 1893 and set about dividing tribal lands into allotments held by individual families. The Curtis Act of 1898 abolished tribal courts and put all residents under the jurisdiction of federal law. And the enabling act of 1906 allowed Oklahoma to draft a constitution.

Approved by voters of both territories in 1907, the constitution allowed citizens to write and submit their own laws to direct vote, permitted voters to accept or reject laws made by the legislature, and prohibited alcohol, a popular social reform of the time. Oklahoma was welcomed as the forty-sixth state on November 16, 1907.

NEW MEXICO

THE LAND OF ENCHANTMENT

January 6, 1912

Capital: Santa Fe	Area: 121,365 square miles	Motto: It Grows as It Goes
Bird: Roadrunner	Tree: Piñon	Flower: Yucca

Missionary Mayhem | The Spanish were the first Europeans to explore New Mexico in the 1500s, naming it *Nuevo Mexico*. Upon learning that the Seven Cities of Cíbola, reported to be kingdoms of great wealth, were actually modest pueblo communities of the Zuni people, the Spanish abandoned plans to settle the region for some time. Missionaries did move to New Mexico to try to convert the Native Americans to Christianity, but were unsuccessful in their attempts to overcome the indigenous religious beliefs.

Juan de Oñate of Mexico was granted a royal contract in 1595 to take possession of New Mexico for Spain. He established the first permanent settlement in San Gabriel. Over time, the Native Americans grew increasingly hostile toward the Spanish. They staged a series of rebellions, but were ultimately conquered and subjected to Spanish rule.

The Mexican War | Inspired by the annexation of Texas in 1845, expansionists demanded annexation of the entire Southwest. Mexico did not recognize the American claim on the land that extended to the Rio Grande, and when U.S. troops were sent to the mouth of the river to enforce the claim, Mexico viewed the move as a provocation. In 1846, President James K. Polk declared war, and the U.S. Army promptly invaded New Mexico.

Did You Know?
The National Fire Safety symbol, Smoky the Bear, was chosen in honor of the cub that was found trapped in a tree during the 1950 fire that destroyed Lincoln National Forest.

Battle at Vera Cruz

General Stephen Watts Kearny took Santa Fe without firing a single shot and claimed New Mexico for the United States. The war ended in 1848 with the Treaty of Guadalupe Hidalgo, in which Mexico formally ceded its land to the United States, including most of Texas, California, Utah, Nevada, Colorado, Arizona, Wyoming, and New Mexico. In exchange, Mexico received a payment of fifteen million dollars. The New Mexico Territory (which included Arizona) was created under the Compromise Measures of 1850, and was therefore open to settlement by both slaveholders and antislavery settlers.

Statehood | New Mexico had to wait sixty-two years to become a state. Opponents in Congress were prejudiced against the large Spanish-speaking population, the so-called wild Native Americans, and the settlers they characterized as inhospitable and uneducated. Finally, with the support of Congress in 1910, New Mexico drew up a constitution and was admitted to the Union as the forty-seventh state on January 6, 1912.

ARIZONA

February 14, 1912

Capital: Phoenix	Area: 113,642 square miles	Motto: God Enriches
Bird: Cactus wren	Tree: Paloverde	Flower: Saguaro cactus blossom

Seven Cities of Cíbola | The name Arizona either comes from the Native American word *arizonac*, meaning "place of the small spring," or is the Spanish interpretation of the Aztec word *arizuma*, meaning "silver bearing." The first Europeans to visit the region were members of a Spanish expedition led by Álvar Núñez Cabeza de Vaca, who were shipwrecked

The Grand Canyon

off the coast of Texas in 1528. They learned of a kingdom from the Native Americans, called the Seven Cities of Cíbola, where the streets were rumored to be paved with gold.

Conquistador Francisco Vásquez de Coronado led an expedition of three hundred men on a two-year wild-goose chase before discovering that Cíbola was a myth. The journey, however, was not all for naught. The Grand Canyon, Colorado River, and Organ Pipe Cactus were all discovered along the way. Few Spaniards returned to Arizona for another two hundred years when silver miners and ranchers began settling the area.

The Grand Canyon | One of the Seven Natural Wonders of the World, the Grand Canyon is one mile deep, two hundred seventy-seven miles long, between four and sixteen miles wide, and six million years old. The downward flowing of the Colorado River is responsible for sculpting much of the Grand Canyon, and the gradual upwarping of the Colorado Plateau has contributed to the majestic effect of the steep canyon walls.

About the year 1850, the U.S. Army made a series of expeditions to survey the canyon and its outlying area. American geologist John Wesley Powell made the first passage of the canyon in 1869, traveling the length of the gorge by rowboat with a small expedition team.

Did You Know?
Meteor Crater is a 570-foot deep, mile-long dent made by a 600-million-pound meteor that struck the earth near Flagstaff fifty thousand years ago. With dust similar to that of the moon, the crater is used by astronauts to train for moon landings.

Statehood | Arizonans began petitioning for statehood as early as 1877, but consistently met with defeat. Once a provision in the state constitution that allowed voters to remove judges from office before the end of their terms was eliminated, Congress admitted Arizona to the Union on February 14, 1912, as the forty-eighth state—the last of the continental states to enter the Union. However, within a year of being granted statehood, voters in the state reinserted the judicial recall article.

ALASKA

THE LAST FRONTIER

January 3, 1959

Capital: Juneau	Area: 570,374 square miles	Motto: North to the Future
Bird: Willow ptarmigan	Tree: Sitka spruce	Flower: Forget-me-not

Land That Is Not an Island | Alaska's first residents were Siberian hunters that crossed a giant land bridge, now covered by the Bering Straits, between twenty and fifty thousand years ago; Eskimo settlements in western Alaska date back to 2000 BC. The first white explorer to discover Alaska was Danish navigator Vitus Bering, who claimed the land for Russia in 1741. The word Alaska comes from the Aleutian word Alyeska, meaning "The Great Land" or "Land that is not an Island." The Aleutian people, living along the western coast and islands of Alaska, were the first to have contact with the Russian hunters.

Although some people were drawn to the region by the profitable fur-trading opportunities with the Aleutians, Russia largely ignored Alaska for the next fifty years. Only when Russian fur companies were threatened by Spanish, French, and English competition did they decide to establish a colony. Three Saints Bay on the island of Kodiak was the first permanent settlement.

Seward's Icebox | After the Civil War, Secretary of State William H. Seward began campaigning for American expansion. He managed to secure the support necessary to purchase Alaska from the Russians in 1867. Having just lost the Crimean War to the British and the French, the Russian government could not afford to maintain the

> **Did You Know?**
> The grueling 1,160-mile Iditarod dog-team race from Anchorage to Nome was started in 1967 to commemorate the famous dog team, driven by Balto, that carried serum in 1927 to break a diphtheria epidemic.

American colony. Baron Eduard Stoeckl, the Russian ambassador to the United States, negotiated with Seward and they drew up the Treaty of Cession—the price for Alaska set at 7.2 million dollars or two cents an acre. Although Seward met with much resistance in Congress, the U.S. Senate voted in favor of ratification by a thirty-seven to two margin. While some Americans approved of the acquisition, many more thought buying Alaska was an unwise decision and disparagingly nicknamed the event "Seaward's Folly" or "Seaward's Icebox." Thirteen years later, Joe Juneau and Dick Harris discovered gold in Alaska, and tens of thousands of Americans changed their tune as they rushed to take advantage of the newfound riches.

William H. Seward

Statehood | Alaska's vulnerability to Japanese and German attack during World War II led the federal government to pour close to two billion dollars of internal improvements into the region. Naval air stations, Army Air Corps bases, the Alaska railroad, and the Alaska–Canada Military Highway were expanded, modernized, and constructed in the 1940s, and thousands of soldiers and construction workers settled in the Alaska Territory.

Although prior petitions for statehood had been made—the earliest in 1916—none were heard in Congress until 1947. A statehood measure passed in the House of Representatives in 1950, but the onset of the Korean War delayed its progress in the Senate. Finally, the territorial legislature approved a constitutional convention and the drafting of a constitution in 1955, and Alaskan voters ratified the document the following year. Delegates lobbied long and hard, and on January 3, 1959, Alaska became the forty-ninth state of the Union.

HAWAII

August 21, 1959

Capital: Honolulu	Area: 6,423 square miles	
Motto: The Life of the Land is Perpetuated in Righteousness		
Bird: Nene (Hawaiian goose)	Tree: Kukui	Flower: Hibiscus

Small Homeland | Polynesians arrived in the Hawaiian Islands sometime between the seventh and thirteenth centuries. They made the two-thousand-mile voyage in long, double canoes. The islands were supposedly named after Hawaii Loa, the first Polynesian man to discover the island chain. Hawaii also means "small homeland." The first white explorer to set foot on any of the islands was England's Captain James Cook, who arrived in 1778. He named the chain the Sandwich Islands in honor of his patron, the fourth Earl of Sandwich; however, the use of the name diminished when the United States began to dominate Hawaii.

Pearl Harbor | Early in the morning of December 7, 1941, the Japanese entered World War II with a massive attack on the U.S. Pacific fleet at Pearl Harbor on the island of Oahu. The devastation that ensued was tremendous—three thousand members of the U.S. Navy and U.S. Army were killed.

Pearl Harbor became the major staging area for American naval activity during World War II because of its prime location in the Pacific. Islanders were subject to martial law for most of the war.

> **Did You Know?**
> The Hawaiian alphabet only has twelve letters—a, e, h, i , k , l, m, n, o, p, u, and w.

Civil liberties were restricted, press was censored, civilian courts were replaced by military tribunals, military officials even controlled workplaces. The nearly one hundred fifty thousand Japanese residents in

Hawaii were immediately mistrusted and treated with hostility. Despite the grilling of thousands of Japanese people by loyalty boards, no incriminating evidence was turned up. In fact, huge numbers of Japanese-Americans volunteered for military service and fought bravely in battle. Two of the most decorated units in American military history were comprised of Americans of Japanese ancestry.

Statehood | Opposition to admitting Hawaii to the Union was initially based on race and national origin—the loyalty of foreign-born residents was questioned, as was the granting of equal status to a mostly nonwhite population. After World War II when Hawaii had proven its mettle time and again, supporters of statehood took up the cause with fresh fervor. In addition, by 1950, most of the territory's residents had been born on American soil. A state constitution was approved in 1950, and on August 21, 1959, Hawaii became the fiftieth and final state to enter the Union.

Japanese attack on Pearl Harbor

COIN
COLLECTING

IN ADDITION TO THE FOCUS ON EDUCATING THE nation about each state's unique history, the 50 State Quarters™ Program aims to reach beyond the established numismatic community in generating public interest in coin design and coin collecting. Known as the "king of hobbies" or the "hobby of kings" because it was originally practiced only by kings and the rich, coin collecting is a rewarding and enjoyable endeavor that can be enjoyed by anyone. The satisfaction gleaned from amassing a complete set of the new quarters is considerable and will be an impressive and lasting achievement to be shared with generations to come. It will require a degree of perseverance to pay attention to the coinage crossing your palm for the next ten years, but the end result will certainly be a source of pride.

Numismatists share a variety of motivations for the hobby of coin collecting—the recreational value of building a collection, the satisfaction of preserving the past, the educational value of learning about the unique stories behind coinage, and the desire to save coins that may bring profit in the future. For numismatic novices, collecting the new quarters is an excellent place to begin the hobby.

As the quarters are circulated by banks through normal distribution channels, in time they will be available to everyone who pauses to examine their pocket change. A fun way to approach the building of a collection is by plucking the most perfect coin of each design and mintmark from circulation. There is a U.S. Mint collector's map and a variety of albums available in which to store and protect your collection. Visit the U.S. Mint website at WWW.USMINT.GOV for further information.

Uncirculated coins, which have been specially cleaned and packaged after stamping, and Proof pieces, which have a more sharply impressed design and a mirrorlike finish, are also available for purchase at a premium for those who prefer to collect these more perfect specimens. The San Francisco Mint produces two different kinds of Proof coins—copper and nickel Proofs, that have the same composition as circulating quarters, and silver Proofs, composed of silver and struck in limited quantities. A complete set of the new quarters would therefore include one sample of each state from the Philadelphia and Denver Mints (indicated by "P" and "D" mint marks respectively), and a copper and nickel Proof, as well as a silver Proof from the San Francisco Mint (both with the mint mark "S".)

A definitive amount of each quarter will be issued, after which the coins will never again be produced, it is a wise idea to get the new quarter during the ten-week period of its being minted. There is no telling just how valuable your collection may become in the future!

The numismatic training and knowledge gleaned from collecting quarters is an excellent introduction to collecting all kinds of other coins. Collections can be organized by series, type, date, or theme. The new quarters would be an example of a collectible series, that is, saving one example of each state coin from each of the U.S. Mint facilities.

A type set of coins consists of one of each major design use for each denomination—for example, there are four types of nickels to collect with a number of varieties that would make the set more complete. Collecting one coin from each denomination by date is another popular approach. Many people choose dates of particular significance such as year of birth or wedding. And theme collections can be amassed by choosing subjects of particular interest like U.S. Presidents or political figures or birds and other animals.

For more information on collecting, storing, and caring for your coins, visit the U.S. Mint website at WWW.USMINT.GOV.

CREDITS

PAGES 6–7: The Picture Collection, New York Public Library; PAGE 7: James A. Simek; PAGE 9: Painting by Edwin Lamasure, United States Mint; PAGES 12, 15–19: James A. Simek; PAGE 20, 22–23: United States Mint; PAGE 26: The Picture Collection, New York Public Library; PAGE 29: "Franklin's Experiment, June 1752." Currier & Ives, © 1876; PAGE 30: Engraving based on painting by Emanuel Leutze; PAGE 33: The Picture Collection, New York Public Library ; PAGE 34: Collection The Connecticut Historical Society; page 36: Greater Boston Convention & Visitors Bureau; PAGE 39: Dan Breitenbach; PAGES 41, 43: Library of Congress; PAGE 45: Colonial Williamsburg Foundation; PAGES 47, 48 Library of Congress; PAGE 51: Title Guarantee Company of Rhode Island; PAGE 53: Charles H. McBarron/US Marine Corps Art Collection; PAGE 54: Engraving from original painting by Chappel. Johnson, Fry & Co. Publishers, 1861; PAGE 57: Private Collection; PAGE 59: U.S. Department of the Interior, National Park Service, Edison National Historic Site; PAGE 61: Library of Congress; PAGE 62: The Picture Collection, New York Public Library; PAGES 65, 67, 69, 70: Library of Congress; PAGE 73: Union Pacific Railroad; PAGE 75: Library of Congress; PAGE 77: The Picture Collection, New York Public Library; PAGE 79: NASA; PAGE 80: The Picture Collection, New York Public Library; PAGE 83: Buffalo Bill Historical Center, Cody, WY; PAGE 85: McKenney-Hall Portrait Gallery of American Indians; PAGE 86: Carleton E. Watkins photo, National Archives; PAGE 89: "Paul Bunyon Swings His Axe." Art & book by Dell McCormick, Caxton Press, 1892; PAGE 90: Illustration by Frederick Remington for "Oregon Trail," F. Parkman, 1892; PAGE 93: From Curtis Botanical Magazine, 1793; PAGE 94: John Steuart Curry/The Kansas State Historical Society, Topeka, Kansas; PAGE 97: Library of Congress; PAGE 99: The Picture Collection, New York Public Library; PAGE 101: Courtesy, Colorado Historical Society; PAGE 102: Library of Congress; PAGE 105: Publicity Division, South Dakota Department of Highways; PAGES 107, 108–109: Library of Congress; PAGE 110: Courtesy of the Montana Historical, photograph by Don Beatty; PAGE 113: "The Rocky Mountains – Emigrants Crossing the Plains," Currier & Ives; PAGE 115: Library of Congress; PAGE 116: Woolaroc Museum, Bartleville, Oklahoma; PAGE 119: Library of Congress; PAGE 120: National Archive/National Park Service; PAGE 123: Engraving based on statue by W. Roffe, "Art Journal," 1877; PAGE 125: Library of Congress